LOVE AND HOPE

Pope Benedict's
Spirituality of Communion

LOVE AND HOPE
Pope Benedict's
Spirituality of Communion

Robert E. Lauder

Resurrection Press
An Imprint of
CATHOLIC BOOK PUBLISHING CORP.
Totowa • New Jersey

First published in April, 2010
Catholic Book Publishing/Resurrection Press
77 West End Road
Totowa, NJ 07512

ISBN 978-1-933066-13-4
Library of Congress Catalog Card Number: 2010924446

Cover design by Geoffrey Butz

Printed in Canada

www.catholicbookpublishing.com

1 2 3 4 5 6 7 8 9

Dedication

To Msgr. Neil Mahoney
(b. 1948 - d. 2007)
"my hero," a friend and dedicated priest
and also to
Karen, Kim, Tara and Kevin Robert,
gifts to all who know them.

Acknowledgments

Grateful acknowledgment is made
to *The Brooklyn Tablet* for
material which appeared previously in its pages.
Special thanks to *Margie DeFelice*
without whose indispensable assistance
this book would never have been completed
and to Emilie Cerar of *Resurrection Press*
whose guidance and encouragement
in bringing the book to publication
have been greatly appreciated.

Contents

Introduction

FOR several years I have been noticing that when I am preaching my remarks often are directed toward myself as well as toward the congregation. What I am preaching not only expresses my interests and, I hope, insights, but it has an almost immediate application to my own life. Not only am I telling those in the congregation what I think is important for them to hear but my remarks turn out to be about what is important for me to hear! How conscious this pattern is on my part, how aware I am when I prepare a homily that I will be saying something about the Christian faith that has a direct application to my own life is not clear to me. The genesis of this book and its theme and content remind me of my experience with preaching. Though I hope others will be helped by what I have written, I know that I have been helped through the writing.

Through two philosophy courses that I teach at St. John's University in Jamaica, New York, some images of God and the human person have changed my way of thinking about both God and us. The two courses are "The Problem of God," which students refer to as "The Problem of Lauder" and "Personalism," a course in which the students and I study insights into freedom, love and commitment from personalist thinkers such as Martin Buber, Emmanuel Mounier, John Mac Murray and Gabriel Marcel. In the course entitled "The Problem of God," even the denial of God's existence by famous and influential atheists such as Ludwig Feuerbach, Karl Marx, Friedrich Nietzsche, Sigmund Freud, Jean Paul Sartre and Ernst Bloch has provided, at least indirectly, insights into the meaning and mystery of God and us. By understanding how many of the more famous atheists did not only deny God's existence but were avid anti-theists, I hope the students and I have been able to purify our notions of God and human persons and gained some knowledge into possible relationships between the Divine and the human.

While the material in the courses both stimulated me and even inspired me, the writings that ultimately moved me to write this book are the creations of two famous contemporary theists, Pope John Paul II and Pope Benedict XVI. By chance, (or was it Providence?), I was invited to be on a committee that was asked to create a spirituality of communion for the Brooklyn Diocese and to link this spirituality to evangelization.

This invitation to be on the committee came from Msgr. Neil Mahoney, a former student and close friend, who died shortly after convening the committee. Neil's life was evidence of the power of a spirituality of communion to foster evangelization. I offer this book as a small tribute to a dear friend and great priest.

Because of my membership on the committee I read carefully Pope John Paul II's Apostolic Letter *Novo Millenio Ineunte* [1] ("At the beginning of the New Millennium") in which the Pope encourages the living out of a spirituality of communion. John Paul's ideas and insights are so beautiful, so illuminating and so obviously relate to some of the truths I had discovered through my two philosophy courses that I knew I wanted to develop and make them more accessible to as many people as possible. Pope Benedict XVI's first encyclical "God Is Love," [2] which I consider a marvelous statement about love and his second on hope, *Spe Salvi*, [3] further encouraged me in my project to help Christians grasp the meaning of a spirituality of communion and perhaps live that spirituality daily. I knew if I tried to help others live it I also would be helping myself live it.

In his Apostolic Letter *Novo Millenio Ineunte* the Holy Father points out that a spirituality of communion helps us to be aware of the mystery of the Trinity living within us and also living in our brothers and sisters. This presence of the Triune God is a gift to us and to our brothers and sisters, and we creatures can become gifts to one another. The Holy Father notes that a spirituality of communion can deepen our membership in the Mystical Body of Christ and help us to share the burdens of others. [4] Obviously a spirituality of communion will call us to be evangelizers, that is, people who wish to share their faith with others. A spirituality of communion calls us to be living signs of the loving presence of Father, Son and Spirit.

Pope Benedict's third encyclical, *Caritas in Veritate*, ("Charity in Truth") [5] applies Christian Revelation and the Pope's profound insights into love to the social order. Unfortunately, *Caritas in Veritate* is not as accessible to a wide audience as his first two letters. Writing in *The New York Times* Peter Steinfels noted the brilliant insights that are present in *Caritas in Veritate* but also noted that the length of the letter and the scope of the topics it deals with make the letter especially difficult reading. Sections of the encyclical contain dense prose and the letter seems cluttered because of the Holy Father's attempt to cover too many topics. Steinfels writes:

"Caritas in Veritate is a document about human nature and the Trinity and the current economic crisis and inequality and the energy problem. It argues a link between Catholic teaching on sexuality and life issues like abortion and Catholic stances on social issues like poverty and the environment." [6]

What struck me most positively in reading *Caritas in Veritate* was how beautifully sections of it illustrate a spirituality of communion. Though scholars may be interpreting and even arguing over some of the Holy Father's statements about various social problems and his application of Catholic social teaching to those problems, it is crystal clear that while details of the letter might be debated, the vision that animates the entire encyclical is a spirituality of communion. The following is the second paragraph of *Caritas in Veritate*:

"Charity is at the heart of the Church's social doctrine. Every responsibility and every commitment spelt out by that doctrine is derived from charity which, according to the teaching of Jesus, is the synthesis of the entire Law (cf. Mt. 22:36-40). It gives real substance to the personal relationship with God and with neighbor; it is the principle not only of micro-relationships (with friends, with family members or within small groups) but also of macro-relationships (social, economic, and political ones). For the Church instructed by the Gospel, charity is everything because, as St. John teaches (cf, 1 Jn. 4:8, 16) and is recalled in my first *Encyclical Letter*,

'God is love' (*Deus Caritas Est*) everything has its origin in God's love, everything is shaped by it, everything is directed towards it. Love is God's greatest gift to humanity, it is our promise and our hope." [7]

This book is a set of reflections stimulated by Pope John's *Novo Millenio Ineunte* but especially by the insights into love and hope in Pope Benedict's three encyclicals, and his book *Jesus of Nazareth*, [8] insights which fit beautifully into a spirituality of communion.

---

[1] *Novo Millenio Ineunte*, at the close of the Great Jubilee of the year 2000
[2] *God is Love* (Libreria Editrice Vaticana, 2006)
[3] *Spe Salvi* (Libreria Editrice Vaticana, 2007)
[4] *Novo Millenio Ineunte*, op.cit.
[5] *Caritas in Veritate* (Libreria Editrice Vaticana, 2009)
[6] *The New York Times*, July 18, 2009
[7] *Caritas in Veritate*, op. cit.
[8] *Jesus of Nazareth* (New York: Doubleday, 2007)

Chapter 1

The Divine and the Human

It all starts with God!

In the course on personalism the students and I discovered that what an individual believes about human persons will affect the view that he or she has about God. This awareness of the relationship between beliefs about human persons and beliefs about God that became more clear to the students and me as we explored personalist philosophy echoed a discovery that other students and I were making in "The Problem of God" course. In that course we found traditional proofs for God such as those offered by Saint Anselm, Saint Thomas Aquinas and Rene Descartes interesting, but equally interesting was the adamant atheism of thinkers such as Feuerbach, Marx, Nietzsche, Freud, Sartre and Bloch. The atheism of these thinkers shed light on both the meaning of the human person and false views of God.

Some of the atheists were correct to reject the god they rejected because that god was a false god. It was not the God that Jesus preached or that Jesus called "Abba." It was not the God Who is totally in love with us and Who calls us into a loving relationship. The god who was rejected by the famous atheists was in one way or another against human beings. It was a god who was made in the image and likeness of the worst in human beings. This false god dominated the consciousness and conscience of human beings and kept some human beings immature and infantile or worse, sick. Each atheist thought that he was liberating human persons from an impossible burden. In a sense each atheist was doing just that. Coming to recognize the false god that atheistic philosophers have rejected can free us to be receptive to the God that Jesus presents to us and invites us to know and love.

Projecting Images of God

Each of us has many images of God. Some images are closer to the truth than others. Some images are so false that they are really terrible. For several years of my life I had a terrible image of God. Unfortunately all of us are tempted to make God in our own image and likeness instead of recognizing that God has created us in His own image and likeness. Both those of us who profess belief in God and those who deny that there is a God can have images of God that are to some extent erroneous. In fact no one can have an image of God that is completely adequate or totally clear. The reason for this is relatively simple: it is impossible for a finite mind to grasp the Infinite; a limited mind cannot adequately grasp an Unlimited Being. God is too much for our minds. This does not mean that whatever we think about God is untrue, but it does mean that whatever we think about God is mysterious. God is Ultimate Mystery. What we think of God may be true but it is never adequate. We can always say that God is *more* and *better* than the images that we have of God.

Reflecting on this, I almost spontaneously think of the philosopher Ludwig Feuerbach (1804-1872), the first atheist that the students and I study. Looking at the histories of religion, Feuerbach noted that images of God had become purified over the years. In the past some people thought of God as the sun or as thunder or lightning but gradually people moved toward a more spiritual understanding of God. Christianity has an exalted vision of God as eternal Spirit and as Father. However Feuerbach insisted that though Christianity's ideas about God are better than material images, all ideas of God are nothing but projections made up by human beings. According to Feuerbach there is no God and when we speak about God we are really only speaking about ourselves. Because we project or place outside ourselves onto another whom we call God something from our own experience of ourselves, we are alienated from ourselves. We are believing in something or Someone who does not exist. When we stop placing our best attributes onto God and realize that all talk about God is really nothing but talk about ourselves, we will no longer be alienated from ourselves. We will know ourselves as we really are. We will be able to appreciate our greatness. Belief in God does not allow us to appreciate ourselves thought Feuerbach.

In their book *Religion and Atheism* William A. Luijpen and Henry J. Koren explain Feuerbach's philosophical vision as follows:

> "Thus the object of religion is within man; God is man's own hidden self and religion is but the solemn unveiling of man's own hidden riches. The religious man doesn't realize at once that his first consciousness of God is consciousness of

his own essence, his first consciousness of God is consciousness of himself as man. For at first man looks at his own essence as something different than himself; he exteriorizes it and calls it God. Only later does he discover that this God is really himself.

"Historically speaking, Feuerbach says, every new, more advanced religion always rejects what its more ancient and primitive sisters adored as God. The more advanced religions disclose that the so-called superhuman contents of the old religions were after all something human, an exteriorization and personification of man's own powers. Fire was a god as long as man stood in awe of it; but no longer when man learned how to make and control it; fertility ceased to be divine when man grasped its workings." [1]

What we can learn from Feuerbach is how much our experience and what we value or fear in our lives influence our ideas about God. All of us to some extent project our ideas onto God but that doesn't mean that God is *nothing but* our human projections. We have to try to purify our ideas about God and not allow our projections to cloud what Jesus has revealed about God. Reflection on how we think about God may help us to see how we project ideas that we gather from our own experience. For example the God who was taught to me in Catholic grammar school and high school religion classes was to some extent a projection. I don't think that my teachers were lying to me but the God who was taught was not the loving Father that Jesus preached. Probably the teachers did not know that they were projecting harsh images of God drawn from their experience of human authority, and for years I did not know that the God I believed in was to some extent a projection of my experience of human authority. That projection made it difficult for me to hear what Jesus has said about His loving Father.

What image of God predominates in my life? That's an important question for each of us to ask. The more truth and depth that is present in images we have of God, the more opportunity we have for genuine human growth, for growth in knowing and loving God. We will never understand the mystery of God completely but that does not mean that we cannot grow in our understanding of God. Some images of God will not call us to growth because they have little or no truth in them. For example, an image of a god who is vengeful or spiteful in relation to us will frighten us but it will not help us to grow and develop as human beings. The image of a god who does not respect our freedom also will not help us to grow. We will never understand ourselves completely but that does not mean that we cannot grow in self-understanding. The more profoundly we understand what it means to be human, the better chance we have of rejecting false notions and images of God. The depth of our understanding of our freedom and of human interpersonal relationships can greatly help us in improving our image of God. This really should not surprise us since our freedom is created by God and we are created in God's image and likeness.

Because of God's loving revelation we have been given entrance into the inner life of God, the loving union of Father, Son and Spirit. As I begin to write about the God revealed to us through Jesus I almost hesitate. The words of the philosopher Ludwig Wittgenstein come to mind,

"About that which we can not speak, we should be silent." Aware of how easy it is to speak incorrectly or inaccurately about mystery, I am reminded of St. Thomas Aquinas' insight that when we speak of God we are trying to speak precisely using vague language. It is very possible to speak truth about God but impossible to say anything clear about God because God is mystery with a capital "M." A finite mind cannot speak clearly about the infinite. Even as seemingly simple and clear a statement such as "God is" could be followed by the statement "God is not the way we are." Thomas Merton said that when those who love God try to talk about Him their words are like blind lions looking for oases in the desert. We can speak of the God revealed through Jesus precisely because God has invited us into relationship. Though I love philosophy and am grateful to many philosophers for insights into the mystery of God and the mystery of the human person, no truth that any philosopher has uncovered can compare to the meaning of God and the meaning of the human person that has been revealed through Jesus. The most marvelous philosophical insights pale in comparison to God's revelation.

A spirituality of communion begins and ends with God. Human history is like a loving breath coming forth from God, a breath that is directed to return to God.

The Triune God

If the notion of the triune God is going to have important meaning in our lives, it has to be rooted in our experience of salvation. Commenting on the experience of the triune God that early Christians had, theologian Elizabeth Johnson wrote:

"In shorthand, we might say that they experienced the saving God in a threefold way, as beyond them, with them, and within them. Accordingly, they began to express their idea of God in this pattern. The New Testament is filled with narratives, confessional formulas, liturgical formulas, doxologies, short rules of faith, all in a threefold cadence. The monotheistic view of God flexes to incorporate Christology and pneumatology. In a word, the triune symbol carries the glad tidings of salvation coming from God through Jesus in the Spirit . . .

". . . The concrete saving ways that God is given to us in history point indirectly to three interrelated ways of existing within God's own life. Trusting that the livingness of God is with us and for us in the suffering of history, we speak of the Trinity as the one true God." [2]

Always keeping in mind that God is radical mystery, we base the entire spirituality of communion in the Triune God. We don't want to approach the Trinity as though we are contemplating and gazing academically, almost disinterestedly, on some eternal distant Deity. No, we come to the Triune God by believing as deeply as we can in the way the Triune God has come to us. One of the best succinct statements about the Living God Who is creating us, the Son Who has conquered sin and death through His own death and resurrection, the Spirit Who animates, inspires and guides us is the following from *The New Dictionary of Catholic Spirituality:*

"All authentic spirituality is *ipso facto* Trinitarian. As such, it is greatly enriched by an appropriate understanding of this central Christian doctrine which lies at the foundation of Christian faith and practice. . . .

"Spirituality considered from a Trinitarian perspective is not anything other than Christian life in the Spirit: being conformed to the person of Christ, and being united in communion with God and with others. Because redemption through Jesus Christ and deification by the Holy Spirit comprise the Christian life, an adequate understanding of Christian spirituality must be grounded in the doctrine of the Trinity. This doctrine functions as the summary of Christian faith, expressing the essential truth that the God who saves through Christ by the power of the Spirit lives eternally in the communion of persons in love. . . ." [3]

In my own formal study of the Triune God and also in my own attempts at living the Christian life, having memorized the doctrine of the Trinity, namely that there is one God, three Persons in God, each Person is God but distinct from the other Two, I was able to articulate the doctrine but really filed it away into some area of my consciousness. Unfortunately, it did not have much of an influence on my attempts at living a Christian life, little influence on either my formal prayer or my day-to-day living. Theologian Karl Rahner might have been speaking of me when he noted that so little does the Trinity function in the piety and faith of the Church that there would cause little stir if it were announced that a fourth person in the Trinity had been discovered. In my own life, with my philosophical background, I tended to look at the Triune

God the way a disciple of the Greek philosophers, Plato and Aristotle, might contemplate, admire and marvel at some eternal truth. That the Triune God, precisely as Triune, should influence profoundly my own relationships was not part of my understanding or practice.

God Is for Us

What has helped me and might help others is the realization that God is *for us*. The real God, the only God, is always reaching toward us, always calling and inviting us, always accessible to us through the Word in the power of the Spirit.

In some contemporary theological reflection on the Trinity three points are emphasized that have helped me. Theologian and spiritual writer Michael Downey, giving credit to theologian Barbara La Cugna, summarizes the three points in the following way:

> "1. . . . whatever is said of the mystery of God must begin by attending to the Incarnate Word, Jesus Christ, and to the presence and action of the Spirit of God in human life, history, the church and the world; 2. The mystery of God is profoundly relational, and this relational mystery is expressed in the language of Father, Son, Spirit; 3. The doctrine of the Trinity is an eminently practical teaching, expressing not only who and how we understand God to be, but what we think human persons are called to be and become: created to glorify God by living in communion with God and with one another through Christ in the Spirit." [4]

In the Old Testament God calls His people. God is love that never withdraws from those who have been called, never negates the call. In story after story God appears as One Who has made a commitment of love, a commitment that is also an invitation to a love relationship. The word "Father" which appears about twenty times in the Old Testament is used, not to suggest a physical parent, but rather one who is loyal, forgiving, constant, merciful. It is used to identify the One Who calls people into a love relationship. It is used to name the One Who wants not a contract, a deal involving rights and duties, but a covenant, an intimate relationship of love.

When Jesus in the New Testament is identified as the Son, it is as the Son of the One who has been called Father. Jesus has a unique relationship with this God Who has made a commitment to people, this God Who is love. When Jesus is called the Word of God this is to indicate that Jesus is God's message, the message and expression of Love itself.

At Jesus' baptism God speaks "This is my beloved Son in whom I am well pleased" as the Spirit descends upon Jesus. That same Spirit leads Jesus into the desert to be tempted and eventually to the cross and resurrection. This Spirit, given to Jesus' followers, is the Breath of God, the Sanctifier. God's plan is that what the Spirit accomplished in Jesus is to be accomplished in Jesus' followers.

Reflecting on a spirituality of communion, reflecting on the amazing truth that we have been invited to enter into the unfathomable love that is the communion of Father, Son and Spirit, reminds me of the statement of author Ronald Rolheiser: "If this is true, it is too good to be true!" [5]

While the terms "Father," "Son" and "Spirit" have a special place in Christian teaching, other terms can also be used to express the mystery that is God. Theologians have experimented with many other terms to shed light on the mystery that is so illuminating that it is too much for us to grasp. I very much like insights offered by theologian Michael Himes. Reflecting on the mystery of God, Himes points out that in the First Letter of John the statement that God is Love refers to a special kind of love expressed by the Greek word *agape*, that in order to avoid confusing this special kind of love with other kinds of love that he prefers the term "self-gift." Himes writes the following:

"So, according to 1 John 4:8 and 16, God is perfect self-gift, total giving of self to the other. Consider this: In the classic Christian definition of the meaning of the word 'God,' we do not say that God is lover. Nor do we say that God is one who loves or experiences love or possesses love. We say that God *is* the peculiar kind of love known as *agape*, perfect self-gift. To put this in other words, the First Letter of John claims that if one wants to know how to think about God, God is least wrongly thought of as a particular kind of relationship among persons, specifically the relationship of perfect self-gift. Now, *that* is a remarkable claim: God is least wrongly to be thought of as a relationship, as what happens between and among persons. In fact, that claim appears many times in the collection of earliest Christian documents that we call the New Testament." [6]

Whatever we say of God is going to be inadequate because God is always more and better than our thoughts about God. However I find thinking of God as a relationship of perfect self-gift inspiring. What Father Himes says about God has set me thinking about the importance of relationships and the practice of religion. There was a time in my life when I did not see any connection between religion and personal relationships. In fact I even thought of personal relationships as possibly distracting us from the depth of religion. Certainly friends were permitted but they should not get in the way of God. That view was due partly to the way I was trained and educated.

When I started teaching the philosophy of existentialism many years ago, I learned that the great nineteenth century Protestant existentialist, Soren Kierkegaard, looked upon his relationship with his fiancée, Regina, as a distraction from his apostolate of bearing witness to Christ. In the twentieth century the great Jewish personalist philosopher, Martin Buber, wrote an essay in which he expressed the view that Kierkegaard had misunderstood the nature of religion. Commenting on Kierkegaard's rejection of Regina, Buber wrote the following:

"That is sublimely to misunderstand God. Creation is not a hurdle on the road to God, it is the road itself. We are created along with one another and directed to a life with one another. Creatures are placed in the way so that I, their fellow creature, by means of them and with them find the way to God. A god reached by their exclusion would not be the God of all lives in whom all life is fulfilled." [7]

Buber made the point that instead of being an obstacle

to God for Kierkegaard, Regina could have been the way to God. If I had to make an either/or choice between the two views, I would side with Buber. I now see religion in terms of personal relationships.

God and Relationships

The notion of God as perfect self-gift should color our understanding of all our relationships. In order to clarify and to emphasize what thinking of God as pure self-gift means, Himes writes the following about the Last Supper scene in John's Gospel in which Jesus gives his farewell discourse to His disciples (Jn 13-17):

"The whole discourse is a meditation on love and community. Surprisingly, Jesus does not tell his disciples to love God. He tells them that they must love one another. Indeed, he says that this will be the hallmark which will distinguish them as his disciples (13:35). Once again, the word used is agape, complete gift of self to the other. Jesus tells his hearers that if they love one another agapically, the Father and he will dwell in them. He urges them to continue to live in the love which he and the Father share with one another. Note, please: God is not the object of love, God is the love that exists among Jesus' disciples. One discovers the presence of God by discovering the love that unites the community. That is our highest and best experience of God's presence." [8]

Of course the way that Father Himes is using the word love goes way beyond having a nice feeling. Rooted in the notion of love as Himes uses it is "gift." When we really give ourselves to one another, when we genuinely care about one another, then God is in our midst. This view of love and of God as a perfect relationship of pure self-gift makes me cherish the personal relationships in my life and want to improve them. It makes me want to be less self-centered and selfish.

My view of religion and personal relationships as having no connection has changed dramatically. More and more I see religion in terms of relationships. One way, and it is an important way, of evaluating what we call an individual's "spiritual life" is by examining the individual's personal relationships, especially the individual's friendships. I have come to believe that how we relate to our friends can give us a clue to how we relate to God. For much of my life I just did not see how religiously enriching friendships can be. Our close friendships can reveal God to us and can reveal ourselves to us. Friendships take a great deal of time and energy and they can cause pain but whatever they cost, they are essential to personal growth and to growth in Christian living.

Noting that the language of "Father," "Son" and "Spirit" is present in the New Testament, Himes points out that Augustine used a different terminology and along with Himes I find it a wonderful terminology. Augustine speaks of God as "Lover," "Beloved" and the "Love between them." Himes writes:

"From all eternity God is the Lover who gives Godself away perfectly; and the Beloved who accepts being loved and returns it perfectly; and the Love, the endless, perfect bond of mutual self-gift uniting the Lover and Beloved. From all eternity God is an enormous explosion of agape, self-gift, and it is that self-gift which grounds all that exists. That perfect gift of the divine Self lies at the heart of everything that exists. Therefore, if we are to be like God, we are called to be agapic." [9]

To be called to be "agapic" is to be called to be self-gift, to be called to give oneself away in love. Even philosophically, without any direct reference to the Christian faith, we could argue that to be a human person is to be called to be a lover. I think that can be established by philosophically reflecting on the meaning and mystery of human person. However in the light of Christian Revelation, the call takes on a richer, more exciting and more marvelous dimension. We are called to be like God, called to be like Father, Son and Spirit. It can be breathtaking to reflect on the meaning and the mystery of the Trinity and that we are called to enter into relation with Father, Son and Spirit. Those of us who have received and accepted the good news Jesus brought should try, in whatever way we can, to spread the news to others. Pope Benedict's encyclical "God Is Love" can be read as a marvelous elaboration of how love is at the heart of a spirituality of communion.

Questions for Reflection

1. Can you give an example of how your view of God influences your view of yourself?
2. Can you give an example of how your view of yourself influences your view of God?
3. What is your predominant image of God?
4. Does your view of the Trinity play a large role in your day-to-day living?

5. How does thinking of God as perfect self-gift influence your relationships with family and friends?

[1] *Religion and Atheism*, Pittsburgh, PA: Duquesne University Press, 1971, pp. 55-56.

[2] Elizabeth Johnson, "Trinity: To Let the Symbol Sing Again," *Theology Today*, vol. 54, 1997, p. 303.

[3] Catherine Mowry LaCugna and Michael Downey, "Trinitarian Spirituality," *The New Dictionary of Catholic Spirituality*, A Michael Glazier book, The Liturgical Press, Collegeville, Minnesota, 1993, p. 968.

[4] Michael Downey *Altogether Gift*, Maryknoll, New York: Orbis Books, 2000, p. 12.

[5] Ronald Rolheiser, *The Holy Longing*, New York: Doubleday, 1999, p. 91.

[6] Michael Himes, *The Mystery of Faith: An Introduction to Catholicism*, Cincinnati, OH: St. Anthony Messenger Press, 2004, pp. 6-7.

[7] Martin Buber, *Between Man and Man*, translated by Ronald Greger Smith, New York: The Macmillan Company, 1967, p. 52.

[8] Himes, op.cit. pp. 7-8.

[9] Ibid., p. 8.

Chapter 2

Love

The Pope's Vision of God

How many people read a papal encyclical? The history of the Church in the 20th century includes several encyclicals that had a tremendous impact both inside and outside the Church. Was this because so many people read them or because they received so much publicity? I'll let the historians figure that one out. What concerns me right now is how many Catholics have read Pope Benedict XVI's first encyclical *Deus Caritas Est* ("God Is Love"). This is a magnificent piece of writing that should have an impact both in and outside the Church. The words that come to my mind to describe "God Is Love" are "profound" and "beautiful."

Before the letter of the Holy Father appeared there was some speculation about what his first encyclical might be. Many were surprised that Benedict chose the topic of love probably because they suspected that the first encyclical might be condemnatory of some aspects of the contemporary world. That love was the topic that the Pope focused on was more than a pleasant surprise. The encyclical is both a marvelous instruction and an urgent and exciting call to Catholics to center their lives on what is essential to their faith, namely God's love for persons and God's call to persons to love one another. The opening words of Pope Benedict's encyclical are a quotation from the first Letter of John, "God is love and he who abides in love abides in God, and God abides in him" (4:16). The Pope points out that in the same verse Saint John offers what is almost a summary of the Christian life when he writes, "We have come to know and to believe in the love God has for us." The Pope suggests that these words can express the fundamental dimension of human life. The most important truth about every human being, young or old, brilliant or intellectually challenged, white or black, rich or poor is that God is totally in love with that person. Whatever else we can say about a human person, the most profound truth and the most important truth about every person is that God's love surrounds the person's life.

God does not love a person because the person is lovable; rather the person is lovable because God loves him or her. God's love is creative. Whatever is exists because God loves it. God's love makes what it creates lovable. We do not have to earn God's love, merit God's love or win God's love. It is pure gift. All we need do is accept it. If we do not accept it, that does not mean that God stops loving us. God will never withdraw love. God has made a commitment to the persons whom God has created. We can rely on God's love; we can count on it.

Years ago I made a day of recollection given by a Catholic sister. At one point during the day in one of her talks she said, "God will never love you more than He does at this moment." I was stunned. I asked myself, "If I say more prayers won't God love me more? If I am a better priest won't God love me more? If I stop sinning won't God love me more?" The answer to those questions is "No." God cannot love me more than God loves me at this moment because God loves me infinitely right now. God is totally and unconditionally in love with me. Whatever else is true about me—my height, my weight, my skin pigmentation, my IQ, my sexual orientation, my vocation—the most important truth about me is that God loves me unconditionally. There are no "ifs" restricting God's love, no conditions. God is completely in love with me. Even though I have been a Catholic all my life, spent twenty-four years in Catholic school from kindergarten to seminary and graduate school, the profound truth that God loves me only became central to my self-image and self-understanding late in my life. I have to wonder how many Catholics believe deeply in God's love for them. That love is the foundation of a spirituality of communion.

Pointing out that in the contemporary world the name of God is sometimes associated with vengeance and hatred, the Holy Father indicated that he wanted his first encyclical to be about the love that God lavishes on us and that we should share with others. If we take seriously the Pope's encyclical then there should be renewed energy and commitment in our response to God's love. God's love can transform us into evangelizers. I suspect all of us have observed people who have had a conversion experience, gained a new awareness of God's love for them and eagerly have wanted others to become more aware of God's love for them.

The Holy Father's insights into love are beautiful. When the encyclical appeared, I joked with some students in one of my classes at St. John's University that the Holy Father must have obtained a copy of my class notes. I was pointing out to them that much of what the Holy Father has written about love the students and I at least touched upon during the course on "Personalism."

Almost twenty years ago I created the course on the philosophy of personalism because I thought philosophers such as Martin Buber, Gabriel Marcel, Emmanuel Mounier and John MacMurray had beautiful and inspiring insights into love and commitment and I wanted to make those insights available to the students. Some of the writings of the personalists are not easy to understand but my hope was that through reading and discussion the students and I would be able to grasp the central ideas of personalism. At the time I created the course I almost was unable to get the course approved because one of the deans at the university thought the course was more theology than philosophy. He thought this because all four personalists center their thought on the reality of God. However I believe that their insights can be understood and even accepted by someone who may not be a member of any religion and so their thought qualifies as philosophy, as a study of human experience without a direct reference to Christian Revelation.

Of course that the course proceeds without a direct reference to Christ marks one way that the material in the course differs from Pope Benedict's encyclical, which is based on God's love revealed to us through Christ. Another way that the material differs from "God Is Love" is that the depth and brilliance of Benedict's insights overshadow anything I might teach. Still it's comforting to think that I am on the same page as the Holy Father.

For me one of the most important truths that Benedict presents in the encyclical occurs in the third paragraph. It is the statement in which Benedict states that he wished to "clarify some essential facts concerning the love which God mysteriously and gratuitously offers to man, together with the intrinsic link between that Love and the reality of human love." We can love because God is Love and God has chosen to share Divine Love with us. The most important and most fulfilling human activities are loving and being loved. All other human activities pale in comparison. Those two activities are possible for humans because God is Love and God created us in God's image and likeness. Whether we are married, single, or celibate, all of us are called to enter into the adventure of love. I think of St. John of the Cross' statement, "In the evening of our lives we shall be judged on how we have loved." Love is the great commandment. Some of the greatest thinkers in history have tried to understand why God creates us and shares divine life with us and the only answer that they can come up with is that Love chooses to do this. God did not have to create. God was not forced to create. God "mysteriously and gratuitously" offers to us a share in divine life and love. God's love reaches out to share.

I have heard some Catholics say that since Vatican II the Catholic religion has become too easy. They seem to think that there should be more sermons on sin and that catechesis should stress more a God to be feared rather than emphasizing the importance of love. I have the opposite view. Love, I believe, is very demanding and it always means some type of movement away from selfishness and self-centeredness. It means focusing on the other. Whether an act of love is as simple as opening and holding a door for someone or as dramatic as making a life commitment to someone, it means putting self second. I don't find that easy and so I don't think love is easy. Perhaps people who think loving is easy have confused love with a pleasant emotional feeling. While feelings can be pleasant they often do not have much depth and they can arrive and depart without much control on our part. Love is a free choice. In fact it is the most important free choice that human persons can make. Choosing to love can change the lover. I have seen this illustrated often in the lives of parents. Many husbands and wives become less self-centered and selfish because of the love for their children. They seem to be transformed and able to make many difficult sacrifices for their offspring. Before they were parents such unselfishness, if present, was less obvious. Because of their love for their children they almost spontaneously place their own desires second to the welfare of their children.

Love and the Human Body

Especially attractive in the encyclical are the Pope's views on the mystery of the human body. Noting that the human person is made up of body and soul, the Holy Father points out that if either the material or spiritual dimension of human existence is overlooked or neglected then love will be misunderstood. To aspire to be pure spirit would lead to a loss of the dignity of human person but to deny spirit and consider the body as the only reality would also be disastrous. My own education tended to emphasize the soul at the expense of the body. It tended to be spiritualistic. Jansenism had influenced the view of the body and of sexuality when I attended Catholic high school, college and seminary. There was a time in my life when I could not understand why the resurrection of the body was important. I thought that all that mattered was that our souls reached heaven. My view of the human person was dualistic, that is I thought of myself as made up of two "things," one of those "things" was the soul and that was important, that was who I really was. The other "thing" was the body and that was the cause of most of our troubles. Personalist philosopher Emmanuel Mounier is quite good on how bodiliness is essential to the human person:

"I am a person from my most elementary existence upward, and my embodied existence, far from de-personalizing me, is a factor essential to my personal status. My body is not one object among others, not even the nearest object—for how then could it be one with my experience as a subject? In fact the two experiences are not separate: *I exist subjectively*, *I exist bodily* are one and the same experience. I cannot think without being and I can not be without my body, which is my exposition to myself, to the world, to everyone else: by its means alone can I escape from the solitude of a thinking that would be only thought about thought. By its refusal to leave me wholly transparent to myself, the body takes me constantly out of myself into the problems of the world and the struggles of mankind. By the solicitation of the senses it pushes me out into space, by growing old it acquaints me with duration, and by its death, it confronts me with eternity.

We bear the weight of its bondage, but it is also
the basis of all consciousness and of all spiritual
life, the omnipresent mediator of the life of the
spirit. In this sense, we may acknowledge with
Marx that 'a being which is not objective is not a
being'—immediately adding, however, that a
being which is nothing but objective would fall
short of the full achievement of being, the personal life." [1]

That the Son of God took on a human nature just like
ours would indicate that human bodiliness is good but if
a teacher of religion in a grammar school or high school or
college tends to be Jansenistic, and to see matter as evil or
sex as evil, then it is possible that students will not be
taught a Christian view of the body but rather a view in
which the body is suspect and perhaps the source of evil
actions. One reason that "God Is Love" is a timely contri-
bution in contemporary society is that it states clearly a
proper view of the human body, of sexuality and of love
at a moment in time when there is an enormous amount
of misunderstanding about the nature of person and the
nature of sexuality. A proper understanding of the
Christian view of the body, sexuality and love would
emphasize that Christians should be the most passionate
people, the strongest, most enthusiastic and excited
lovers.

Eros and Love

In Pope Benedict's "God Is Love," philosopher Friedrich
Nietzsche is cited by the Holy Father in his discussion of
eros. The Pope points out that the love between man and

woman was called *eros* by the ancient Greeks but the word appears only twice in the Greek Old Testament and not at all in the New Testament. [2] The New Testament authors prefer the Greek word *agape* when they refer to love. The Holy Father goes on to point out that the Greeks thought of *eros* as an intoxication, a loss of reason, which yielded to a kind of divine madness. For the Greeks *eros* was celebrated as a divine power and found its expression in fertility cults and part of this was prostitution practiced in temples. The Pope indicates that the Old Testament opposed this form of religion and though it saw this as a perversion of religiosity, it did not reject *eros* totally but only this distortion of it, a distortion which takes away the dignity of *eros* and actually dehumanizes it. Such a distortion of *eros* led to the exploitation of the women who served as temple prostitutes. Indicating that *eros* needs to be disciplined if it is going to lead to more than fleeting pleasure, if it is going to lead to the happiness for which every human being yearns, the Holy Father believes that a refined *eros* can lead us to God. Christians should not be less erotic but more erotic, not less passionate but more passionate. Everything that we think of as beneficial in the Christian life, everything that is supposed to help us grow as Christians—commandments, prayers, fasting, studying, spiritual direction, sacraments—is to help us love. We are on a lifelong journey, an adventure in grace, in which we are called to fall more deeply in love with God and be more loving toward our neighbor. An *eros* that is properly directed, will indeed give us a taste of the divine, a glimpse of heaven because it will deepen our union with Father, Son and Spirit. *Eros* should be at the center of a spirituality of communion but the Pope believes that a "growth in maturity" is called for if we are going to direct *eros* toward God. The Holy Father is calling us to a deeper way of living, one that is a sign of faith precisely because it is erotic, that is based on a deep and passionate love.

I very much like the Pope's insistence that "growth in maturity" is called for if we are going to direct *eros* toward God. More than one hundred years ago Nietzsche announced to Christians that they really did not believe in God, that the idea of God was dead for them. In 2006 the Holy Father called us to a deeper way of living, one that is a sign of faith precisely because it is erotic, that is based on a deep and passionate love.

Eros and *Agape*

When he was a professor of theology, Pope Benedict must have been a wonderful teacher. I surmise that the Holy Father was an excellent teacher because of the logical order in which he presents his ideas in "God Is Love" and also the way through repetition and review that he emphasizes certain ideas and seems concerned that readers will understand exactly what he is presenting.

Discussing the history of philosophical and theological debate about the nature of love, Pope Benedict notes that often a distinction has been so emphasized between two types of love that the two loves have almost seemed to be antithetical. One love, which has been called descending love, *agape*, typically identified as Christian, has been contrasted with the ascending, covetous and possessive love, *eros*, which has been referred to as non-Christian and typical of the love emphasized in Greek culture. The Holy

Father is concerned that if this distinction between ascending and descending love is overemphasized, it would isolate the essence of Christianity from relations that are fundamental to human living. While descending love, that is Christian love, would be very admirable, it would be cut off from the fabric of human living. The Pope is correct to be concerned about such an isolation, such a narrowing of Christian love, a depiction of Christian love that would have little if anything to do with the struggles and difficulties that human beings have as they try to love. A primary goal of the new evangelization is to speak to people's experience. When Christians talk about love they must speak truths that speak to people's experience of love.

We have to learn to love. We are made for love, for loving and for being loved, but that does not mean that our love is perfect. Some of us as we try to reach out to others in love can be possessive, and dominating, and manipulative. As love progresses the person ought to become less and less self-centered and more and more centered on the other. However, for most of us this does not come about easily. For most of us it is a journey, sometimes a journey that lasts a lifetime.

The Holy Father states that in love relationships one must be ready to receive. This, I think, is an important insight. I feel awkward when someone compliments me. I tend immediately to make a joke. This is a fault. We should be able to receive the sincere compliments of others just as we should be ready to admit that we need the love of others. No one can just give, give, give. We are finite and needy. We come to reach the fullness of personal existence through the love that is bestowed on us by

others. Think of the love that has been lavished on us by
our parents. For most of us our parents are the most influential persons in our lives.

Human existence is an adventure in love: we are created by Love and our goal is eternal union with Love. The
Pope's descriptions of how God loves us and what the
love relationship between God and us is are literally
breathtaking. As a kind of preface to his comments on the
vision of love presented in the Bible, the Holy Father
points out that the Bible gives us a new image of God. In
cultures surrounding the Jewish people the image of gods
was unclear and even contradictory. With the development of biblical faith the view of God became clearly articulated in the prayer that was fundamental to Israel: "Hear,
O Israel, the Lord our God is one Lord" (Dt 6:4). Noting
that there is only one God and that God created all that is,
the Pope points out that creation is dear to God, that God
loves human beings, that the God of Israel has a personal
love for people. Developing themes that he has touched on
in earlier sections of his encyclical Benedict stresses that
the love that God has for people is both *eros* and *agape*.

How often do we think that God is passionate toward
us? Any notions we have about a disinterested God, a distant God Who observes our lives from some heavenly
pinnacle, could not be further from the truth. Our God is
passionately in love with us. The passion of great lovers
immortalized in literature, theater and film pales in comparison to God's love for every human person. God's passionate love for us goes beyond our imaginations' ability
to picture or our minds' capacity to conceptualize.

But the Pope points out that God's love, God's *eros* for
us is also totally *agape* and he suggests two reasons for

saying this. One is that God's love for us is completely gratuitous, completely gift. We do not have to earn God's love, merit God's love or win God's love. God's love brings us into being out of nothing and makes us lovable. The second reason that the Pope offers for claiming that God's love is *agape* is that it is a love that forgives. The Holy Father says that this forgiving love "is so great that it turns God against himself, his love against his justice." That is truly amazing. When we sin, God's justice should demand our punishment but God goes "against himself" and forgives.

Images of God and Us

One of the themes that Pope Benedict deals with in his encyclical is the relation between the biblical vision of God and the biblical vision of human person. How we think of God will play a role in how we think of ourselves and how we think of ourselves will play a role in how we think of God. This became obvious to me when teaching the two courses, "The Problem of God" and "Personalism." Referring to how God is depicted in the Old Testament, the Pope notes that God is shown as the absolute and ultimate source of all being but also shown to be a lover with the real passion of true love.

When the author of the "Song of Songs" wanted to write about the intimate union between God and human person the author used sexual imagery, the imagery associated with human sexual love. Perhaps sexual imagery was the best that the author could do. Obviously the author is not claiming that God's love for people is exactly like the love that a husband has for his wife but the author is implying that this is the best imagery that can be employed to indicate how intense and strong and passionate God's love for us is.

Equally interesting is the Pope's insistence that the union with God is the primordial aspiration of the human person whether an individual knows that or not. God has made us for union with God and nothing less is ever going to fulfill us. Saint Augustine was stating a profound truth when he wrote that our hearts will be restless until they rest in God. But Pope Benedict insists that the union is not one in which we lose our identity. It is not a fusion into the Divine. We do not become God. In fact through this union with God we become more ourselves, our personal identity is strengthened. This is amazing. Love is the only union in which identity is not lost but rather increased. In human sexual love between a husband and wife the husband becomes more himself and the wife becomes more herself. There is no union except love in which the identity of the two beings is not lost. Not only is it not lost, the identity of each is strengthened.

If a human lover can help me to be more myself, then a love relationship with God would seem to hold out infinite possibilities for the human person to grow and develop, to become more free and more loving. Pope Benedict XVI grasps this deeply. Through "God Is Love" the Holy Father wants to spread the message to us. Discussing marriage, Pope Benedict stresses that in the story of Adam and Eve the idea is present that man is somehow incomplete, that man is driven by his very nature to seek in another the part that can make him whole. The Holy Father points out that the creation story indicates that it is through communion with the opposite sex that man can become "complete."

Two aspects of the story of the creation of human persons are emphasized by Pope Benedict. The first is that *eros* is essential to man's very nature. To be a man is to be a seeker, one who leaves parents in order to find a woman and with a woman to become "one flesh." The second aspect, equally important in the view of the Holy Father, is that *eros* moves a person towards marriage, toward a unique and definitive bond and it is only in this bond that *eros* fulfills its deepest purpose. This is truly a beautiful image of marriage. Married couples are to be like God loving His people. This is both inspiring and challenging!

The depth of Benedict's vision of love is revealed when he writes about Christ. Noting that there is a deep union between the two Testaments forming the one Scripture of the Christian faith, Benedict indicates that what is really new about the New Testament is not that it presents new ideas but that it presents the figure of Christ and because of Him the ideas about love take on an unprecedented realism. [3] The novelty of the Old Testament was not merely in its beautiful ideas about love but in its insistence that God acted out of love on behalf of His people. This love takes on a new form in the Incarnation of God's Son. Noting that the novelty of the Old Testament did not consist merely in abstract ideas but in God's unprecedented activity, the Holy Father notes that Jesus' parables tell us something profound about God. What is revealed in Jesus' parables is that God is pure self-gift. The God Who appears in Jesus' parables is so much in love with us that the love cannot even be conceived by us. The image of the shepherd going after the lost sheep, the woman looking for the lost coin and the father going out to meet the prodigal son suggest something of God's love for us but

God's love is always more than we can imagine. A spirituality of communion is all about love. It is about recognizing God in each person and that we are called to share joy and sufferings and friendship. A spirituality of communion helps us to see others as gifts and to allow that vision to influence how we relate to others both locally and globally.

Love and Eternity

Early in "God Is Love," the Holy Father referring to the Old Testament Book the "Song of Songs" or the "Canticle of Canticles," suggests that it reveals a profound view of love. [4] Noting that the book was well known to the mystics, Benedict notes that according to the interpretation that is generally held today the poems contained in the book originally were love-songs. They may have been intended for a Jewish wedding feast and the intention behind them was to exalt conjugal love. Certainly the Holy Father also exalts conjugal love in his encyclical.

What especially interests the Pope is that in the book two different words in Hebrew are used to indicate love. One word seems to indicate a love that is still searching, somewhat insecure. The word used for this is the Hebrew work *dodim*. This word is plural and is eventually replaced by the Hebrew word *ahaba*. The Greek version of the Old Testament translates *ahaba* as *agape* and earlier in the encyclical the Pope has pointed to us that *agape* is the word preferred by the New Testament authors to convey the meaning of love. In contrast with an insecure love, a love that is still searching, the word *ahaba* suggests a love that has discovered the other, a love that moves beyond selfishness. The word indicates concern for the other, care for the other. Rather than self-seeking, this love wishes the good of the one loved. Unlike the love suggested by the word *dodim*, this love is ready to sacrifice.

Two points that the Holy Father refers to in order to stress love's growth are extremely important: exclusivity and eternity. It is no secret that marriage in this country is in a crisis situation. The last statistic that I heard concerning marriage was that two out of three marriages break up. How can this be? What is wrong? I know that in trying to prepare couples for marriage I emphasize the importance of communication but I often find that prospective marriage partners do not seem to share on a very deep level. In fact I wonder what some couples talk about when they are together. Recently a very reflective couple told me that the months preparing for their wedding were a terrible experience. They were forced to be preoccupied with trivia. They told me that in the year before their marriage the time they spent with me was the only time that they spoke with someone about what was really important in married life. If their experience is typical, that is really sad.

I very much like the Holy Father explicitly relating love to eternity. [5] Belief in life beyond the grave reveals in a special way the great dignity and value that a human person has. If persons did not live beyond the grave I would be forced to confess that human existence was absurd. There is no experience that can rival the death of a loved one. There just is no other experience like it. The death of a loved one raises all sorts of questions about the meaning of human life and the meaning of love.

I have a great respect for the atheistic existentialist philosopher Albert Camus. He seems to have been a person who had great compassion for the poor and suffering. However his denial of a life beyond the grave seems to me to diminish greatly the dignity and importance of human persons. The Roman Catholic existentialist philosopher Gabriel Marcel believed that love for another person revealed the immortality of the one loved. He was correct. If I wish to know someone as deeply as possible I must love that person. Loving enables the lover to perceive what non-lovers miss. Loving gives special vision and I believe part of what that vision provides is the awareness that the beloved will live forever. In linking love to eternal life the Holy Father is touching upon what is most basic in Christianity. It is also basic to a spirituality of communion.

Questions for Discussion

1. Do you think that love is a feeling?
2. What do you think of the Pope's view of the human body?
3. What is the difference between *eros* and *agape*?
4. According to the Pope what is love's definitive goal?
5. How is God's love for us erotic?

---

[1] Emmanuel Mounier, *Personalism*, Notre Dame: University of Notre Dame Press, 1952, p. 11.

[2] *God Is Love*, op. cit., sections 3-5.

[3] Ibid, sections 12-19.

[4] Ibid, sections 6-8.

[5] Ibid, section 12.

Chapter 3

Risen Life

Resurrection and Human Experience

How we think of God and the human person will affect how we think of the Risen Christ and of course how we think of the Risen Christ will affect how we think of God and the human person. What is happening between the Risen Lord and those who meet Him in New Testament stories? Though we will never understand the Risen Christ while we are on this earth, we want our images of Christ and of the risen life to which we are called, to be as meaningful as possible. If risen life is the life to which all of us are called, then prayerful reflection on this great mystery can be profitable for our faith, our hope and our love. Prayerful thought about the Risen Christ can inspire us, encourage us and move us to be more zealous in trying to spread the Good News.

A spirituality of communion, like any Christian spirituality, has to give a central role to the Risen Lord. What do we mean when we say that Jesus rose from the dead, appeared to many of His disciples and lives among us today? The Resurrection of Jesus of Nazareth was the central and decisive event in the lives of His followers. In the light of it the Scriptures were written and the sacraments celebrated. It should also be the central event in the lives of Jesus' followers in the 21st century.

Insights from theologian Dermot Lane can be helpful in our efforts to probe as deeply as we can into the mystery of the Risen Christ and to relate the mystery to our own experience. After studying all the New Testament texts that mention appearances of the Risen Christ, Lane offers a person-to-person transforming experience as one way to think about the encounters that followers of Jesus have with Jesus in His risen state. I like the model of an inter-personal encounter that Lane offers. It moves between two erroneous views, one that would say that the experience of the Risen Christ was totally subjective, meaning that the encounter was created totally by faith, and the other totally objective, which would say that the encounter was accessible to anyone, that faith was not needed. The model of a person-to-person transforming experience makes the presence of the Risen Christ real but able to be encountered only through faith. Lane writes the following:

". . . the resurrection appears not as some exception or isolated incident but rather as the realization and crystallization of man's deepest aspirations. The resurrection of Jesus from the dead is not just a fake nor is it some kind of trick that was suddenly pulled off at the last moment to salvage a hard-luck story, nor is it a violation of the laws of nature. Rather the resurrection is, in the case of Jesus, the full realization and actu-al fulfillment of those seeds of indestructibility which exist within the heart of every individual.

It was the blossoming forth of these seeds of indestructibility within the whole man Jesus after death that the apostles were trying to communicate, in proclaiming the resurrection of Jesus from the dead. It would have been impossible for the apostles to make such a bold and extraordinary claim unless they had been compelled to do so by a real experience of the living, personal, and transformed presence of Jesus after his death." [1]

The Risen Lord whom believers encountered in the New Testament stories is the same Risen Lord whom believers today encounter in the sacraments, in their prayers and in their daily experience of living as Christians. The encounters that happened two thousand years ago dramatically transformed those who had them. That should encourage us to approach the sacraments with enormous trust and confidence.

Our belief that the goal of human living is to participate in the life that Jesus through His death and resurrection has won for us gives our lives a direction. To put it succinctly, our belief that we are moving toward the fulfillment of risen life means not only that we are not adrift in a meaningless universe but that we are moving toward an existence that is so wonderful that we cannot imagine it clearly or comprehend it completely. It is too marvelous, too magnificent. The goal of human living puts our most exalted dreams to shame. Our dreams and desires cannot come close to the wonderful fulfillment that God has arranged for us. A spirituality of communion can remind us of this and move us to spread the Good News.

To claim that risen life cannot be completely understood by us is not to claim that it has no meaning at all. Religion should speak to our experience. The concept of risen life does speak to our experience, it can illuminate all our experiences. In thinking about the truth that all persons are called to risen life beyond the grave, I have been helped by Otto Hentz's marvelous book *The Hope of the Christian.* Recognizing that the resurrection is a mystery, Father Hentz notes that it must nevertheless somehow fit our experience. Claiming that it does, he notes that each of us wants to experience the fullness of life and the fullness of beauty and love. He writes the following:

"Further, we hope that our lives will be meaningful in some definitive way, beyond the flow of open-ended, indefinite time. There are many questions that we *have*, and there is the question which we *are.* The question that we are keeps us constitutionally restless until we get caught up into the fullness of meaning, beauty, and love. Hence our openness in hope for the future is not openness to just this or that event. It is openness to the event of resurrection. The notion of resurrection speaks to the deepest desire and hope at the heart of us. It makes sense.

"There is a circularity in our faith in resurrection. On the one hand, there is in us an elemental hope that opens us to news of resurrection. On the other hand, the news of resurrection clarifies the hope it satisfies. . . . If we are disposed to reverence the human person as having a depth that is infinite in capacity and reach, the notion of a resurrection event will not seem bizarre, a primitive myth. In turn, news of the resurrection sum-

mons us to appreciate the reach at the heart of us
as a hope for eternal life, and so clarifies the hope
that alerts us to accept the news." [2]

Each of us is searching for fulfillment. We want more
meaning in our lives, more beauty, more love. You cannot
be human and not desire more of these most important
realities. Our society does not encourage us to be reflective but when we do reflect we know that we want
human fulfillment; we want our deepest desires to be met.
The resurrection means that our deepest desires will be
met. Hentz is correct in stating that there is a circularity to
our faith in the resurrection. Looking at the deepest levels
of ourselves we discover that we are creatures of hope. At
times we settle for immediate gratification but when we
seriously reflect on our lives we know that no material
possession is going to fulfill us. There is a profound need
within us that no thing will fulfill. Our deepest need will
be fulfilled by risen life. If we are aware of how profoundly needy we are, then we will be ready to receive the
good news of risen life. A spirituality of communion
simultaneously calls our attention to our poverty and
neediness and also our richness and greatness because of
the Triune God's loving presence within us.

The Bodily Self

For much of my life, as I mentioned earlier in this book,
I had a dualistic view of what a person is. I thought a person was two things, two realities: a body and a soul
instead of one being with two dimensions. The difference
between thinking of a person as a soul who has a body
rather than thinking of a person as a single reality that has
two dimensions may seem academic, the sort of thing that

might interest philosophers and theologians but that has little importance for the lives of most people. The "practical" implications of how we think of ourselves might not be immediately evident. Actually how we think of the bodiliness of a person has important implications for how we think of resurrection and how we think of God's call. Pope Benedict's social encyclical, *Caritas in Veritate*, stresses the importance of communion among human persons even here on earth. The full communion that will happen beyond the grave begins on earth among bodily beings.

There was one point in my life when I could not see what was so important about the resurrection. What seemed important was whether my soul reached heaven. I really did not see why I should be concerned about the body as long as my soul made it to paradise. Thinking this way was a distortion of the Christian message. Without realizing it I was embracing the dualistic philosophy of Plato rather than the Christian message. The Greek philosopher Plato looked down on matter and believed that matter dragged us down, that matter was responsible for most of our problems and that at death we were fortunate to be freed from our bodies. This is to miss drastically the materiality of the human person. Whatever else we are, we are material. Christian faith concerning the resurrection is different from belief in the immortality of the soul. Theologians point out that in Sacred Scripture the concept of person does not involve a distinction in a person of two different parts. Rather Sacred Scripture portrays person as one being having two dimensions. When one word is used to convey one dimension what is being named is the whole person. So when St. Paul writes about flesh and spirit he means to refer to the whole person with either word. For St. Paul flesh does not refer to the body and spirit does not refer to the soul. Rather flesh refers to the whole person who is sinful and spirit refers to the whole person living in grace.

How we think of our bodiliness influences how we think of ourselves being called by God or at least to what we think God is calling us. Thinking of the perfection of the person as being disembodied implies a view of person that is individualistic and this carries over into how we think of ourselves in relation to God and to other persons. The resurrection of Jesus reveals that we are not called to be disembodied. We are called not to be isolated individual souls but to be bodily persons who are called to be members of a community both here in this world and in the fullness of God's Kingdom beyond the grave.

The resurrection implies that any spirituality that might be characterized as a "me and Jesus" spirituality is not adequate to what God is accomplishing in us. The entire human community is being called to risen life. No one is excluded from God's loving plan. The history of salvation is the history of God calling a people, of God shaping and forming a people into a community of love. The contemporary emphasis in Catholicism on social justice and on contributing to the building of the Kingdom of God does not spring primarily from sociology, anthropology or psychology but from belief in what the resurrection means.

Words that can be quite confusing in relation to the faith are "proof," "evidence," and "reasonable." We cannot prove the Christian faith. By a proof I mean an argument, to which when it is grasped by the mind, the person must assent. The individual has no choice once he or she grasps the argument. We are not free to say that two plus two equals thirteen. Our minds see that two plus two equals four and a person must admit that. However to say that the Christian faith cannot be proven is not to say that there is no evidence to support the Christian faith. There is a great deal of evidence starting with the witness of the apostles and others who experienced the presence of the Risen Christ shortly after His death up to the fact that the meaning of the Christian faith speaks to the deepest needs and desires of the human heart. Though the Christian faith cannot be reached and affirmed by reason without God's grace, the Christian faith ought to be reasonable. It ought to make sense. It is not silly nor does it contradict our experience. Father Hentz is quite good on this point. He writes the following:

"Revelation fits our experience. Though it tells us something we do not figure out on our own, the revelation, when heard, rings true. This is not surprising since the revelation is for us and for our salvation. It would make no sense to us unless it somehow speaks to our experience, meets some elemental human need and desire. On the one hand, revelation clarifies our hope. On the other hand, examination of our experience clarifies how revelation responds to our hope for a fullness of life.

"Similarly, our present experience allows us to anticipate, however inadequately, the what and the how of the end time. The yearning to move beyond what frustrates or hurts us to find full and definitive completion of what we can most fully be—that yearning helps us understand the substance of our hope. We also know from our experience the elemental dynamics of human living that move us toward fulfillment. Through analysis of fundamental human yearning and the dynamics of personal living, illumined by God's revelation in Christ, we can elaborate the general shape, the plot lines, of what we anticipate for our ultimate future.

"Of course, reflection on what we anticipate in the present cannot add new information to God's promise of eternal life or provide concrete details about the shape of the ultimate future. Reflection on what we anticipate in the present provides a way to understand that promise." [3]

I love Hentz's statement that revelation "rings true." God's revelation to us, which is God's self-gift through the incarnation of the Son of God, can tell us the most profound truths about God and about ourselves. Revelation speaks to us on the deepest level of our being. It illuminates for us the most profound meaning of human living and dying. All the great thought systems pale in comparison to God's revelation to the human race. The best response to God's revelation is "Thank You."

Hope should play a role in our lives, even in our day-to-day living. We are very future oriented. When we call a person a "not -yet," a "self- transcender," a "self-project," an "openness to the future," we are using expressions that professional philosophers use to capture a fascinating aspect of the human person. All these expressions are attempts to articulate that a person is not finished but is oriented toward the future. The reason that the expressions are awkward is that they are terms trying to capture adequately the mystery of person. The most dynamic person is directing himself or herself toward the future, the most lethargic person is directing himself or herself toward the future. For better or worse we are directing ourselves toward the future.

Because we are oriented toward the future, we are creatures of hope. Each of us has hopes and dreams. Some hopes and dreams may be quite unrealistic. We usually reserve the term "dreamer" for someone whose feet are firmly planted in midair. Some hopes may not call forth the best in us because we have set our sights too low. What we deeply hope for plays a significant role in the type of person we become. If we reflect on our hopes, we may be able to discover a great deal about ourselves. Our hopes can reveal to us what type of person we are. Father Hentz links hope to the nature of person. He writes the following:

"Created in the image and likeness of God, summoned by our very nature to union with God, the human spirit is a dynamic capacity for the infinite. Our reach for the infinite, therefore, is not a particular activity alongside other human activities. The reach for the infinite is at work in all human activities, each of which is a limited expression of the deepest reach of the human spirit, the reach to God. . . .

"It is because the human spirit is a boundless capacity measured only by the mystery of God that in everything apart from God we experience limitation and must live in hope. The hope at the heart of life is hope in God as the ultimate one who embraces our history in self-giving love.

God, the Creator, can draw all things together in unity. God can guarantee the ultimate meaning of human life in the world by allowing our lives together to share in the infinite life of God." [4]

We are made for God. Every hope we have even if it does not explicitly focus on God, implicitly is for God. Nothing less than God is ever going to satisfy us. We desire truth. We cannot stop asking questions. We desire to commit our lives to something important. We desire to be unconditionally loved. All these desires point toward God. What human living is all about, even if some persons do not know it, is communion with God. We are magnetized by God, drawn by God. Our goal is union with God. Nothing less than God will fulfill us. We have many hopes and desires but they are for objects which are relatively dim images of God. Everything that appeals to us has an attraction for us because it "looks" like God, is a creature of God and therefore participates to some degree in God's beauty and attractiveness. A spirituality of communion excludes no one. We are called to be in communion with God and with our brothers and sisters. Thinking about the call that each person receives from God can strengthen our sense of community. On every level of being human—the intellectual level, the emotional level and even the spiritual level—we depend on other people. For better or worse we are deeply influenced by others.

We depend on other people intellectually. I can teach philosophy at St. John's University only because I had the opportunity to study at the graduate level and had some wonderful teachers who helped me understand the great philosophers. Whatever value my teaching has is due to a great extent to the fact that I have read books and articles which were penned by very gifted and talented people. For my knowledge of the contemporary world I depend on newspapers and television commentators. Whatever truth I grasp about current events is filtered through other persons. From pre-school through grammar school, high school, college, seminary, graduate school right up to this morning's daily newspaper, I have relied on the intelligence and honesty of others.

We depend on each other emotionally. The founder of psychoanalysis, the psychiatrist Sigmund Freud, thought that from the ages of three to six we are tremendously influenced emotionally by parents and others who are significant in our lives. In fact Freud thought a person's basic emotional personality was fixed for life by the time he or she was six years of age. Though I do not agree with Freud, I admit that we are greatly influenced emotionally by others when we are young. We are also influenced emotionally by others throughout our lives. If I spend all my time with sad, cynical people, I will find it difficult to be happy and optimistic. If I spend all my time with happy, optimistic people, I will find it difficult to be sad.

We are also influenced spiritually by others. This seems especially mysterious to me. Only Christ saves us but within God's plan we can be helped or hindered by others. In God's Providence everyone will have the opportunity to accept redemption and salvation. No one will go to hell because of what someone else has done nor will anyone be saved by anyone but Christ but we can be positively or negatively affected by others. I think of Mother Teresa. She inspired millions of people. The great saints have influenced millions. Jesus' mother Mary has influenced countless numbers of people. If a person lives in a parish in which there are great preachers and in which the liturgy is celebrated beautifully and devoutly, then that person will receive benefits that someone who lives in a parish in which the homilies are terrible and the liturgy is celebrated poorly does not receive. No one is going to be cheated by God but we can play important roles in the lives of others. We can be gifts to them and they to us. To the extent that we think of ourselves as souls rather than a mysterious union of matter and spirit, we can miss the importance of community in the Christian life. The central role that community has in Christianity is more evident if we emphasize that we are incarnate spirits, persons who have two dimensions, a material dimension and a spiritual dimension.

Risen Life and the Human Community

Being part of God's Kingdom means we genuinely care for others. If we are called by God to be gift-givers, and everyone is, then it is important that we serve others in any way that we can. There are many problems in the world and they probably will not go away unless people solve them. No one person can do everything but every person can do something. As we are called into a deeper love relationship with God, we are also called into service of others. On one occasion after I gave a talk someone paid me one of the nicest compliments I have ever received. The person said, "You use your talents well to help the community!" Members of a community even by their neediness can communicate God's call to us. This is fascinating. Not only by their gifts do the members of a community help us but by their poverty they can help us.

God's call often comes to us through members of the community. We can hear God through the needs of our brothers and sisters. A spirituality of communion helps us to "listen" to the gift that each person is.

I think of poverty in two ways. The first way I would categorize as poverty in relation to possessions. The second way I would categorize as poverty on the level of being. The first is easy to understand; the second is impossible to understand completely. Poverty in relation to possessions refers to people lacking what they need to live a decent human life. It might mean that they are starving or that they do not have a decent place to live or that they have so little that they cannot attain a good education. It might also mean that they have some of the necessities to live but lack the resources that would enable them to develop as persons, that their poverty prevents them from growing and reaching their human potential. To be in a community with such people, as all of us are because we are human and have brothers and sisters all over the world, is to be called by them. Their poverty on the level of possessions is a call to us to do what we can for them. Each of us has to examine his or her conscience and decide just what we can do for those of our brothers and sisters who have almost nothing.

Poverty on the level of being is the type of poverty that every person has. To be a person is to be needy. What is it we need? We need other persons. More specifically we need to be loved by other persons. Everyone does. Babies, who are washed and fed and clothed but not loved, die. That is amazing. All of a baby's physical needs can be satisfied but if the baby is not loved, the baby dies. Being loved is what helps us to grow as persons. The self-made man is a fiction. The person who does not need to be loved does not exist. To be a person is to need to be loved. That is the way that God made us. Some persons may not know how important it is to be loved. They may think that they are self-sufficient. They are wrong and to the extent that they live out their false belief their lives will be disastrous.

If we recognize that persons need to be loved we can take that need as a call from God. It is often through the neediness of other persons that God calls us. I think of a poem by an anonymous author that I once came across. As I recall it consisted of the following three lines:

I sought my soul but my soul eluded me.
I sought my God but my God I could not see.
I sought my brother and I found all three.

The neediness of other persons can help us see that we are called to give ourselves in love to others. Some do this in marriage, others as celibates, others in the single life. Members of a community can help us discover more deeply who we are. We are persons created by God to love. Whatever state of life we are in, whatever our specific vocation, we are called by God to live lives of love.

Everyone is called by God into an intimate love relationship. Catholics are called, members of other Christian denominations are called, Jewish people are called, members of Islam are called, agnostics are called, atheists are called, all people are called. No one is excluded or forgotten. This call, which is mediated to us in an ultimate way through God's Son, can reach us through many channels. The call is constant. God never stops inviting us into a relationship. Though ultimately the call comes through Christ, it can be mediated through human persons and if we are attentive and reflective we can experience the call in our daily lives and in what we may think of as ordinary experiences. One of those experiences, which is anything but "ordinary," is the experience of loving and being loved.

The gift dimension of loving is one of the strongest signs of God's loving presence in our lives. Love is a free self-gift. We can think of any love relationship and it always involves a free self-gift. In effect one person says to another person or to a group of persons "I am for you." Some degree of unselfishness is involved in every act of love. Any love relationship might be used to illustrate unselfishness. The unselfishness characteristic of parental love especially impresses me. To me parental love is phenomenal. Two people have a baby and they give, and give, and give so that some day that baby is free enough to say, "Goodbye." That to me is an extraordinary expression of love. Frequently lovers tend to be possessive. I know that I am tempted to do this with my friends. Lovers try to own the beloved. Parental love calls the parents eventually to let go. In fact the entire love relationship is to help the child stand on its own two feet, to become more free, to become independent. We know that some parents are not good at this. They become possessive. They think they are helping but they are really hurting. Somewhere along the son's or daughter's way to adulthood the parents have to allow the offspring to be free. That cannot be easy. At what age do the parents allow their offspring to be on his or her own? Figuring that out must be one of the great difficulties of being a parent.

What especially interests me about parental love, and indeed all genuine love, is the unselfish aspect. From where does that come? The unselfish aspect of love has its roots in God's unselfish love for us. Our faith tells us that the ultimate source of being is unselfish love, that God is pure self-gift. We have many images and ideas about God and some are better and closer to the truth than others but the best image is that God is pure self-gift. There are many signs of God's unselfish loving presence in our lives. One beautiful sign is an act of unselfish love by a human being. When we encounter or observe such an act, we can be reminded of God's loving call, perhaps even experience at least indirectly, God's unselfish call. All unselfish love is ultimately due to the presence of the Risen Christ and his Spirit in our lives, moving us toward the Father. A spirituality of communion is rooted in unselfish love.

Questions for Discussion

1. How does theologian Dermot Lane suggest that we view the experience of the Risen Lord that Jesus' disciples had?
2. What is the connection between personal fulfillment and risen life?
3. What is the difference between a "private spirituality" and a "personal spirituality"?
4. "Revelation fits our experience." What does that statement mean?
5. What do we mean when we say that we are summoned by our very nature to union with God?

---

[1] Dermot Lane, *The Reality of Jesus*, New York, Paulist Press, 1977, pp. 64-65.
[2] Otto Hentz, *The Hope of the Christian*, Collegeville, Minnesota: A Michael Glazier Book, The Liturgical Press, 1997, pp. 59-60.
[3] Ibid, p. 39.
[4] Ibid, pp. 15-16.

Chapter 4

The Eucharist: A Special Presence

Prayer and Presence

For much of my life the great problem I have had with praying is preventing my prayers from becoming routine. I have found myself thinking of prayer in terms of an obligation that I had to fulfill rather than a visit with the Lord. Somewhat thoughtlessly, I, from time to time, have allowed my prayers to become some kind of duty that I had to perform, something I had to "get in" every day rather than a normal, natural outflow of my relationship with God.

Recalling different periods in my life I wonder if some problems that I have had with prayer are due to an irrational fear of God. At times, there may have been a real hesitation to become close to God because of some unfortunate images I had of God from childhood and teenage years. Of course I cannot be certain but I suspect that those images hindered me from speaking to God in a personal way, from experiencing God as the God of love Who wants an intimate, loving relationship with me.

During a recent vacation I had an interesting experience. For more than twenty years, I have engaged in centering prayer by setting aside 15 or 20 minutes each day (the time is arbitrary). You try to focus on the presence of

God. As you engage in centering prayer, you try to forget what you have been doing before the prayer and not think about what you are going to do when the prayer is finished. You are not making prayers of petition. You are just being with the Lord in silence, enjoying God's presence in your life, focusing on God's presence in the center of your being. You start the prayer by composing yourself, trying to be relaxed in God's presence. Then you pick some word or phrase that is meaningful to you and you say it silently in rhythm with your breathing. For example, you might say "My Lord and my God." Eventually, as you experience the closeness of God, you might choose to stop saying the words and just enjoy God's presence. If you become distracted, you might choose to start saying the word or phrase again. At the end of the 15 or 20 minutes, you conclude the prayer by slowly and devoutly reciting an Our Father.

There were two experiences that I had during a recent summer vacation that are related to my doing the centering prayer. First, I found that I was more relaxed while saying it and was not as easily distracted. More than once during vacation I had a clear sense of God's presence, a stronger sense of the Person in whose presence I was placing myself. Second, I found that during the remainder of the day I was less preoccupied with problems, less anxious. Of course, this might be attributed to the fact that I was on vacation, but I think it was due to my experience of the centering prayer. I am not suggesting that we make prayer a giant aspirin or a small valium. Prayer is not therapy. But I suppose I should not be surprised that if our prayer becomes more personal, our daily lives will change.

For years, I found a definition of prayer that I probably learned from a catechism quite satisfactory. It seemed to apply to Our Fathers, Hail Marys, private prayer, prayers of petition and even to the Mass. The definition was, "Prayer is the raising of the mind and heart to God." However, I no longer think of it as the best way to describe prayer. My problem with the definition is that it suggests that prayer starts with us. It gives the impression that we pick ourselves up by our own bootstraps and turn ourselves toward God. I now believe that prayer starts with God. Prayer, any kind of prayer, could not happen except that God reaches out to us, calls us into relationship.

The description of prayer that I now prefer is, "Prayer is hearing and responding to the Word of God." This applies to all prayer. Every prayer starts with God's initiative. God speaks to us, and we respond. I don't mean to imply that we literally "hear" God's voice. The word of God is God's Son, Christ. This Word is ever-present in our lives, calling us, inspiring us, sanctifying us. When we respond to the presence of Christ, then we are praying.

If the description of prayer that I now prefer is correct, prayer might be happening in all sorts of situations and in all sorts of actions that we might not usually think of as prayer. When we visit a sick person in a hospital, that might be a prayer. When we attend a wake for the deceased, that might be a prayer. When we forgive someone, that might be a prayer.

Sometimes priests, religious, and devout lay people wonder if they pray enough. Looking at their busy schedules, they might think that they do not allow sufficient time for prayer. I believe that, if a person is trying to follow Christ, that person probably is praying often. An individual might not be thinking of Christ and yet still be responding to Christ's presence in his or her life. When I studied theology, we used the term "actual grace" to explain why a person performed good actions. We would say that God sent an actual grace, and the person responded. I believe that "grace" is just another term for God's loving presence.

Of course, besides the actions that I am describing as prayer, there is also what we usually refer to as private prayer. This might take the form of Our Fathers or Hail Marys, or it might be in words less formal that we spontaneously choose. In *Jesus of Nazareth*, Pope Benedict writes the following:

> "This is what prayer really is—being in silent inward communion with God. It requires nourishment, and that is why we need articulated prayer in words, images, or thought. The more God is present in us, the more we will really be able to be present to Him when we utter the words of our prayers. But the converse is also true: Praying actualizes and deepens our communion of being with God. Our praying can and should arise above all from our heart, from our needs, our hopes, our joys, our sufferings, from our shame over sin, and from our gratitude for the good. It can and should be a wholly personal prayer. But we also constantly need to make use of those prayers that express in words the encounter with God experienced both by the Church as a whole and by individual members of the Church." [1]

There is great wisdom present in the Holy Father's insights. The more we allow God's presence to suffuse our being, the more capable we will be to be present to Him. In other words, God's presence within us opens us up to relationship with God. The more present we are to God, the more God's presence will fill us. There is a kind of rhythmic interaction between God and us. It is important that we remember God starts the relationship. What response can we make other than loving gratitude?

There is a danger that we evaluate our prayer life in excessively narrow ways. For example when we engage in prayers of petition, if what we ask for is not granted then we think our prayer did not "work." I suggest that prayer can "work" in a broader and more important way than merely achieving for us some particular favor or blessing that we want. In fact it is impossible that prayer not "work." Prayer, especially daily prayer, can change the way we look at our lives and the lives of others. If our prayer is sincere and personal, it can deeply affect our outlook. People I know who seem to be people of prayer spontaneously look at life and life's problems from a special point of view. Their faith seems real and seems to color many of their judgments.

Each person has some vision of life, some vision of what reality and especially human living means, what the purpose and goal of human existence is. Some philosophers and theologians refer to this as a person's horizon. The metaphor of "horizon" is a good one. Visually the horizon is as far as you can see. When we refer to a person's horizon we are referring to what is meaningful to that person, what matters to that person, what is important and relevant to that person. For example calculus is not part of my horizon. I have never taken a calculus course and I really have no idea what calculus is. Calculus is not one of the meanings that matter to me.

There are many factors that go to make up an individual's horizon. Parents and family can be very influential. Schools attended, friends, and in our time especially the media have a strong influence on a person's horizon. The newspapers and magazines we read, the television and films we watch can have a strong role in shaping our horizon. I think daily prayer can deeply influence a person's horizon. The more personal the prayer is, the more it comes from the heart, the stronger will be the influence on the person's vision of reality and on the person's grasp of what human life is. Daily personal prayer can deeply affect an individual's understanding of what the purpose and goal of human existence is. If we come from God and our ultimate fulfillment comes from union with God beyond the grave, then we should not be surprised that prayer makes more clear to us who we are, who God is and how we are supposed to live to reach our ultimate goal.

There are many activities that can help us to grow as human beings. Physical health and psychological health are important. Education can be a wonderful help. Decent living conditions are also a plus. Every person is like a planted seed that should grow and develop. Because human persons are free, our own decisions play a crucial role in our growth or decline. How we pray is one of the most important decisions that we make.

How we pray not only has a profound influence on how we live but it can also reveal how we think of God and how we think of ourselves. Prayer ought to be at the center of our lives and its presence or absence says a great deal about ourselves and about how we think of God. I find interesting the fact that many people I meet and talk with have an image of holiness which they probably received when they were children. The image suggests that being holy is being pious, living in some ethereal realm removed from the daily mundane chores that preoccupy most humans. According to this understanding of holiness, the truly holy person is probably in some monastery or convent cut off from the secular city that the rest of us inhabit. Most of us would smile or even laugh out loud if someone described us as holy. Even to think that we should try to be holy seems strange to many. Yet isn't this what each of us is called to be? There is no human activity, except sin, that cannot help us grow closer to God. The world is charged with the presence of a sanctifying Spirit and only sin can cut us off from that Sanctifier. Prayer puts us in touch with the Spirit Who is always lovingly reaching for us.

Called to Be Holy

I suggest that the first step toward answering God's call to be holy is to look at our prayer life. Certainly that is the first step that I need to take. Whatever shape my formal prayer takes each day, what is crucial for me is that I be present to God as personally as I can be. That is how God is present to me.

I teach a course "Philosophy and Literature" and the course has two subtitles: "Meaning, Mystery and Metaphysics in the Catholic Novel" and "God, Satan and Sin." In the course there is a great deal of class discussion because I believe that this is one way to provoke the stu-

dents to think deeply about what is in the novels. Two
topics that come up for discussion every time I teach the
course are the nature of holiness and what it means to call
someone a saint. I am not surprised because all eight of
the novels that the students are required to read in the
course deal with these two topics.

The eight novels that we deal with in the course are
Graham Greene's *The End of the Affair* and *The Power and
the Glory*, Evelyn Waugh's *Brideshead Revisited*, Shusaku
Endo's *Deep River*, George Bernanos' *The Diary of a
Country Priest*, Walker Percy's *The Moviegoer*, Mark
Salzman's *Lying Awake* and Ron Hansen's *Mariette in
Ecstasy*. Though some of the books do this more than others, each novel can raise questions about holiness and
sainthood. My experience teaching the course and having
discussions about these topics is that many students have
what I think of as a narrow understanding of holiness.
Some think that saints are less than human, others that a
saint must be some perfect specimen of humanity. In one
of the novels one of the characters is promiscuous but
before she dies she makes a loving leap of faith to God
and seems after her death to be performing miracles
among those whom she knew on earth. Some of the students have a tough time accepting that a sinner can
become a saint. The character in the novel does not fit
their image of a saint and they have difficulty believing
that such a person can become a saint.

Both what we believe about prayer and how we experience praying can remind us that each of us is called to
holiness, that God calls each of us by name. Sinners that
we are, God wishes to have an intimate loving relationship with each of us. Though that can seem mind-bog-

gling, it is the truth. That we believe this as profoundly as we can is important. This awareness can influence all our other religious beliefs and put them in a proper context. God is all for us. In his excellent essay "Accessible Holiness," Father William O'Malley, S. J. emphasizes that among the creatures on earth we are unique in our being called to holiness:

"What separates humans from other animals is the potential to learn and to love. Other animals know facts; a stag pursued by hunters knows that danger is behind him, but so far as we know he does not ask why: 'What did I do to those guys?' We have at least the capacity (if we use it) to understand. Other animals can give their lives for their young. But we can give our lives (often without dying) for people we do not even like at the moment. Ask any parent or teacher. Can we entertain the possibility that our God-given purpose is to prepare a fully realized recipient for the gift of holiness? Nor is that role limited to purging defects, as so many were taught, but more importantly to amplify those potentials of knowing and loving. . . .

"If God is content that an individual is trying his or her best (for the moment) to fulfill God's hopes in raising humans above animals, that person qualifies as a saint, even if the Vatican has not gotten around to ratifying God's judgment." [2]

If someone is trying his or her best then of course that person is close to God, which is another way of saying that the person is holy and a saint. One of the important ways that we can prepare ourselves to be "a fully realized recipient for the gift of holiness" is through our formal prayer. If we are inviting God, Who has already invited us, into a personal relationship then how could we not grow closer to God and so at least for the moment, be holy? We are not on our own. We are not picking ourselves up by our bootstraps when we try to fulfill God's plan for us. God has initiated the process. God has called us into relationship.

Can we say that God is dependent on us? Even as I write that the Infinite, the Unlimited, has become vulnerable I am in awe. I suspect that only love could accomplish this. We Christians certainly do not believe in a distant God. Rather, we believe God has become one of us, put Himself at our disposal, placed Himself in our hands. We can spend our lives meditating on this action that God has taken in relation to us, and I doubt if it will ever lose its capacity to stun us and make us awestruck. When we have some awareness of God taking a chance on us, risking Himself in the face of our freedom, putting Himself at our disposal, how can we help but respond with love? When God creates free persons, God takes a chance, God risks that free creatures may not do what God wants, indeed may do the opposite of what God wants.

In this relationship that we have with God, when we pray to God, it is impossible that our prayers go unheard or unanswered. In *Jesus of Nazareth*, Pope Benedict stresses what the most important gift that God gives us is when we ask for something. The Holy Father writes:

". . . the gift of God is God himself. The 'good things' that he gives us are himself. This reveals in a surprising way what prayer is really all about: It is not about this or that, but about God's desire to offer us the gift of himself – that is the gift of all gifts, the 'one thing necessary.' Prayer is a way of gradually purifying and correcting our wishes and of slowly coming to realize what we really need: God and his Spirit." [3]

The notion that what we need more than anything is God is profoundly true. This insight that prayer, any type of prayer should gradually help us to purify and correct our wishes and slowly to realize that what we need is God is terribly important. For many of us this awareness may not come easily but all prayer should help us to move toward that awareness. Prayer can help us to see that no other reality can compare to the God Who loves us and invites us into relationship.

God wants to communicate with us and wants us to communicate with Him. If we can appreciate this, our prayer life should benefit greatly. Among other advantages we receive by being aware that God wants to dialogue with us is that we are reminded that we can have absolute confidence in God being present throughout the moments of prayer. Never is prayer a solitary activity. Whether we seem to be alone in a church or in a room in our home, no one is alone when he or she is praying. God is always present in prayer and not just as the one Who is addressed. We can have confidence that not only are we communicating with God but God is communicating with us.

God starts the prayer process. We are called by God, invited by God, summoned by God. Without this initiative on the part of God, prayer could not happen. Because we are called by God, we can respond. We have been given the privilege, the grace, to call God's name.

Whether the prayer is a Eucharist or an Our Father or a few words spoken at bed time, the basic process of prayer is the same: God takes the initiative and we freely respond.

In *Jesus of Nazareth*, Pope Benedict comments on the Our Father and stresses how reciting the prayer can change us, can form us and shape us as we grow into our vocation of being God's children. We are being drawn into being sons and daughters of God by Christ. The Pope writes the following:

"This gives the concept of being God's children a dynamic quality. We are not ready-made children of God from the start, but we are meant to become so increasingly by growing more and more deeply in communion with Jesus. Our sonship turns out to be identical with following Christ. To name God as Father thus becomes a summons to us: to live as a 'child,' as a son or daughter. 'All that is mine is thine,' Jesus says in his high-priestly prayer to the Father (Jn 17:10), and the father says the same thing to the elder brother of the Prodigal Son (Lk 15:31). The word father is an invitation to live from our awareness of this reality. Hence, too, the delusion of false emancipation, which marked the beginning of mankind's history of sin, is overcome. Adam, heeding the words of the serpent, wants to become God himself and to shed his need for God. We see that to be God's child is not a matter of dependency but rather of standing in the relation of love that sustains man's existence and gives it meaning and grandeur." [4]

Being a child of God has a dynamic quality to it. There is an expression that I have heard people use when something that they planned did not work out the way that they wanted. The expression is, "God is not finished with me yet." I think that everyone of us can believe that the statement can be applied to us. None of us is a finished project. Each of us is on the way toward the Kingdom. Our journey is not one that we take alone. The Holy Spirit, the Spirit of Christ, not only accompanies us on our way but leads us on our journey. Our task is to respond to the promptings of the Spirit.

To grow in relation to the Father, to grow into the vocation of being God's children, does not mean that we become more and more dependent but the opposite. It means that we grow into the freedom of the sons and daughters of God. Whatever particular shape or role our vocation to relate to God as Father takes—married, single, celibate—we ought to grow in freedom. We are called to lives of love, and the more free we are, the more we can love. Many experiences can foster our freedom. I believe that education offers special opportunities for growth in freedom. Formal prayer has a special power to free us, to liberate us, and help us grow as persons and as children of a loving Father. Encountering God is a most liberating experience.

Eucharist and a Spirituality of Communion

Everything that has been written in this book is related to the Eucharist. This is the family meal that makes a spirituality of communion possible. God calls us together in the Eucharist. All prayer is precious but *the* perfect prayer is the Eucharist. This is because it is the Risen Christ's prayer. The Risen Lord is offering Himself to the Father and we are privileged to join in that prayer. Every Eucharist is offered to the Father, through the Son. The Holy Spirit makes our participation in the offering possible. This great action has to be central to any spirituality that is Catholic.

When I was a young priest I frequently described the large number of parishioners who did not attend Sunday Mass regularly by saying, "They have the faith, they just don't practice it." I would never make such a statement today. Of course no one but God knows who does or who does not "have the faith," but I have come to see the Eucharist as so central to Catholicism that I tend to identify being a Catholic at least partially with celebrating a Sunday Eucharist. I cannot think of anything more essential about being Catholic than worshiping at the Eucharist. In the Eucharist everything that we live as Catholics is stated and not only stated but acted out in union with the Risen Christ.

In "God Is Love," Pope Benedict beautifully relates the mystery of the Eucharist to the mystery of love. [5] The Holy Father insists that in order to understand Jesus' teaching on love we must relate it to the Eucharist. Noting that the ancient world had some notion that what really nourished human persons was eternal wisdom, Benedict points out that this wisdom has become food for us as love. Through the Eucharist we are drawn into Jesus' offering of Himself. What has to be emphasized today, especially in a culture which promotes individualism such as ours does, is that the Eucharist not only unites us with Christ but also with other persons. The Pope makes a special point of this. He insists that we cannot possess

Christ just for ourselves because communion draws me not only toward Christ but toward unity with all Christians. The Holy Father knows that we become one body and that God comes to us bodily so that He can continue His work both in us and through us.

I would have to write another book in order to present a commentary on the Pope's insights into the mystery of the Eucharist and love of neighbor. There is so much there. What I think deserves special emphasis is the truth that there is no such thing as a private relationship with Christ. By "private" I do not mean personal. Every relationship with Christ is personal. A private relationship would be exclusive of other people. St. John tells us that if we say we love God and do not love people, we are liars. Once a person gets involved with Christ the person necessarily gets involved with others for whom Christ died. To get involved with Christ is to enter a community. To get involved with Christ is to inherit brothers and sisters.

The Eucharist is not a private prayer. It's the prayer of Christ and his Mystical Body which is all of us. Supposedly it was the Irish author James Joyce who said "Catholicism means here comes everybody!" I love that statement and it applies especially to the Eucharist, which is a love meal. As the Holy Father wrote, it is no wonder that the word *agape* has been used to describe the Eucharist. If we examine the texts of the Mass, we will see that everyone is included in our prayers. We can bring our private and personal intentions to the Eucharist but the meaning of the Eucharist will call us to a love not just for our family and our friends, or even just for those who have asked for our prayers. I also believe that those who are deceased and now with Christ are present at Mass. Of course I believe that Mary and canonized saints are at the Eucharist, but I also believe that my father, mother and sister are at the Eucharist. I realize that this is difficult to imagine or picture but it is true. Those who have loved us while they were alive on earth love us at least as much now that they are with the Risen Lord and are at least as present to us as they were before their death.

Every so often in reading a book I find that something seems to leap off a page and engages my attention and interest completely. When this happens, I find that I am almost forced to stop reading momentarily and think about what I have read, and yet I want to read more and learn more about the insight that I have encountered. Sometimes the text reminds me of something else that I have read that also caused me to pause and reflect. I had this experience while reading Bernard Cooke's *The Future of Eucharist: how a new self-awareness among Catholics is changing the way they believe and worship.*

Mentioning that there are many things that influence how a person interprets experience, Cooke notes that beyond all those realities lies something that can only be known by faith, and he calls this the sacramentality of a person's experience. Discovering and accepting the sacramentality of experience, Cooke believes, will affect a person's involvement in the celebration of the Eucharist. He writes the following:

"Very briefly, because God is present and active in people's lives, those lives are a 'word' about this God. Actually, for each of us, our own experience of ourselves as we go through the days and years of our life is the primary word that tells us about God in relation to us. I may be

well acquainted with the Scriptures and their
message about God in relation to humans; I may
be well educated about traditional Christian
teaching about God; but what more than anything else tells me about God in relation to me is
my experience of being me. That basic word is
often ambiguous and needs interpretation. It has
depths that only faith, guided by Scripture and
Christian teaching, can discover. Yet in that deeper discovery we come to believe the unbeliev-
able: God is for us in profound friendship.

"As we become more aware and open up to
the gift of God's self, the divine presence trans-
forms the entirety of our life. What this means is
that the 'ordinary' elements of our experience
carry God-meaning, something that runs counter
to the prevalent belief that God intervenes only in
extraordinary events. . . . However, we are more
aware today that God is present in the 'ordinary,'
in our loving and being loved, in our dealings
with one another. Because God is so present, our
lives in their entirety—most specially in those
ordinary things that are part and parcel of every
human life—take on a new depth of meaning.
This is another way of saying that our lives are
sacramental to the degree that we become aware
of this involvement of the divine with us." [6]

Cooke goes on to say that it is this sacramentality that
is being celebrated when we gather for the Eucharist. That
the primary word about God is myself amazes me. Yet
this makes sense if God is completely involved in my life.
Because God has chosen to be present to me as long as I

am human, in other words as long as I am I, it follows that to think about God is also to think about myself, and to think deeply and correctly about myself is to think about God. Of course, I am not God; but my humanity, my very identity, is tied to God's presence. The commitment God has made to me is irrevocable.

I think in his book, *Doing the Truth in Love: Conversations about God, Relationships, and Service,* Michael Himes makes the same point that Cooke has made about the self, though Himes uses different terminology. Noting that everything is potentially sacramental, Himes suggests that the fundamental sacrament for each person is that very person. Each of us is called to affirm himself or herself. Himes writes:

> "The primary sacrament for you is your self, as the primary sacrament for me is my self. The beginning of true holiness, the discovery of the sacramentality of the universe, is to be able to look in the mirror and say, 'I know how radically limited that creature is, and it is good.' This is no small thing; it may be the work of a lifetime— to affirm the goodness of your existence, not as an ideal, but as you concretely are. It is the revelation of the fundamental sacrament. Once you see yourself as sacramental, as rooted in grace, as good, then the sacramentality of everything else lights up. And until one can see one's self as sacramental, I do not think that one can ever appreciate the sacramentality of everyone and everything else." [7]

Michael Himes is stressing the same point that Bernard Cooke stresses. To see oneself as sacramental is not pride or conceit. It is seeing reality the way it is. It is affirming God's creation and redemption of oneself. I am reminded of lines from my favorite poem, Gerard Manley Hopkins' #34, *As Kingfishers Catch Fire:*

> *I say more: the just man justices;*
> *Keeps grace: that keeps all his goings graces;*
> *Acts in God's eye what in God's eye he is—*
> *Christ—for Christ plays in ten thousand places,*
> *Lovely in limbs, and lovely in eyes not his*
> *To the Father through the features of men's faces.*

One example of Christ playing in 10,000 places, the Eucharist calls us to commitment and to communion. Sister Carol Frances Jegen, BVM, has summarized, beautifully, the power of the Eucharist in our lives:

"Every Eucharist reminds us that we need continual nourishment in this life of loving. Every Eucharist sends us forth to share God's life of compassionate love, especially with those who are suffering. Every Eucharist enables us to experience some of the joy Jesus promised in his Last Supper Discourse. 'I have told you this so that my joy may be in you and your joy may be complete' (John 15:11). Every Eucharist enables us to enjoy more fully a life of friendship with God and with one another. Every Eucharist joyfully celebrates our oneness in God's tripersonal loving through, with and in Jesus. Every Eucharist enables us to share life more vibrantly with our loving tripersonal God who is continually making all things new." [8]

Questions for Discussion

1. How is centering prayer related to God's presence?
2. Is the Pope correct in saying that prayer is really silent inward communion with God?
3. Is it true that there are no unanswered prayers?
4. Is God dependent on us?
5. How is the Eucharist related to a spirituality of communion?

---

[1] *Jesus of Nazareth*, op.cit., p. 130

[2] "Accessible Holiness," *America*, July-August 2007, p. 21.

[3] *Jesus of Nazareth*, op.cit., pp. 136-137.

[4] Ibid., pp. 138-139.

[5] *God Is Love*, op.cit., sections 13-18.

[6] Bernard Cooke, *The Future of the Eucharist: how a new self-awareness among Catholics is changing the way they believe and worship*, New York: Paulist Press, 1997, pp. 43-44.

[7] Michael Himes, *Doing the Truth in Love: Conversations about God, Relationships and Service*, New York: Paulist Press, 1995, p. 109.

[8] *Transformed by the Trinity*, Chicago: Loyola Press, 2008, pp.98-99.

Chapter 5

Commitment and Communion: Reaching Out to Others

Love in Action

In the second half of his letter "God is Love," Pope Benedict writes about the Church's charitable activity. What the Holy Father is stressing is that love must be put into action. What Christians mean by love and what our society often promotes as love through the media is quite different. The image of love that comes through the media often seems quite weak, even selfish and self-centered. If we take the insights of the Pope seriously the view of love that he has offered is almost exactly the opposite of a selfish or self-centered depiction of love.

The most important truth about each person, the basic identity of each person, is that God loves him or her. While this love is pure gift, meaning that we do not have to earn it or merit it or win it, nevertheless accepting God's love for us does have implications. We should reach out in love toward others. Because we are sinners and tend to be selfish, we often find reaching out to others in love difficult and demanding. The stress in the Catholic faith on the importance of love does not make being a Catholic easy but it does make being a Catholic an absolutely beautiful way of living.

So central is love to the life of a Christian that Saint Augustine, as Pope Benedict mentions in his encyclical, "God is Love," was able to write, "If you see charity, you see the Trinity." That is amazing. When we love, we reveal the Trinity to one another. The Blessed Trinity is a perfect communion of love. There are many ways that God is revealed to us. God can be revealed through history, through nature, through art. One of the most important ways, and certainly one of the most powerful ways, is through love. When we love we are like God. When we love we speak God to one another. We are made in the image of God and we never image God better than when we love. When we love we are revelations of God to one another.

In stressing that the Church must be involved in works of charity if she is to be what God intends her to be, the Holy Father writes in "God is Love" of the central role of the Holy Spirit in the life of the Church and refers to the Spirit as the energy at the heart of the community. I find the image of the Holy Spirit as energy exciting. The image I have is that love is animating us, moving us, driving us. The energy surrounds us with love, inflames us with love. Our experience of this energy makes us want to share it with others. Love is the mystery at the root of all human activity, the center of everything important that we do. To refuse to accept love and to refuse to give love is to reject the meaning of being human.

If the Holy Father is correct in writing that the entire activity of the Church is an expression of a love that seeks the integral good of man then that provides a model of human living for each of us. In whatever way that we can we want to promote the growth and development of people. Depending on our vocations, we will do this differently but the basic vocation which all of us share is being called to love. It is love that is at the heart of what is being called "the new evangelization."

In *Caritas in Veritate* the Holy Father stresses the relationship between truth and love. We must search for truth and place what we discover into the "economy of love" and also discover what is true about love and reject any false sentimentality which might be tied to a relativistic understanding of truth. Relativism suggests that we invent truth rather than discover it. [1] Certainly anyone who teaches contemporary college students experiences how widespread relativism is. In every philosophy course I teach I begin by helping the students see that relativism is a self-contradictory position: if there is no objective truth then the view that there is no objective truth is not an objective truth!

Call to Commitment

There is very little in our culture that encourages life commitments. A popular view is that life commitments prevent people from growing, that they prevent or stunt personal development by closing off future options. Change is so pervasive and often so quick in our society that life commitments almost seem anti-human. What a person thinks about life commitment, whether it is possible or not and whether it is desirable or not, involves that person's interpretation of human life, indeed of all of reality. What a person thinks about life commitments also involves what a person thinks about human freedom and about God.

Whenever I officiate at a marriage I am in awe at the commitment that the two people are making. I think it is amazing that one person can love another person so much that he or she is ready to say in effect, "No matter what, no matter how life treats us, I am for you forever. You can count on me." I am so in awe of that kind of love and trust that I am tempted to say "You're kidding!" when either the man or woman expresses in words the marriage commitment. I have never done that but it is tempting because I think it is mind-boggling that two people can love one another so much that they make vows for life.

Of course in the fifty years that I have been a priest I have come to see that some people have entered marriage without realizing the seriousness of what they are doing. As someone who is not married I am always amazed when I find a husband and wife who do not seem to know one another at all. I wonder what their dating experience was and I wonder what they share after they are married. Do they reveal themselves to one another? Do they share their deepest thoughts and feelings?

Some married couples have had a wonderful experience in renewing a marriage commitment. To observe couples who have found a deeper meaning in their marriage can be a beautiful experience. Their renewed commitment can be an inspiration and channel of grace to others. Many people who have made the "Marriage Encounter" report that the experience helped them to revitalize their marriage, helped them to reach a new level of communication. When I was a young priest and a couple came to me with a serious marriage problem, I thought that my task was to help them fall in love again, help them to renew their commitment. With some couples this did seem to happen. However I have to wonder whether some who have serious marriage problems ever made a deep commitment. Listening to some describe their relationship, I wonder if there was ever anything substantial in their relationship.

Anything that can be done to encourage life commitments, to foster and nourish them should be done. The health or lack of health of a society can be evaluated in relationship to the strength of the life commitments in that society. Our personhood develops through life commitments. This is how we grow emotionally and spiritually. This is how we grow in our relationship with God. Making life commitments is not easy. Understanding life commitments completely is impossible!

I can recall an incident several years ago in which I gave a talk to a group of people, several of whom were not Catholic. After the talk a woman came up to me and asked "Why did you become a priest?" I took her question very seriously. For some time I had been thinking about vocations and more specifically vocations to the priesthood. However vocations were not the topic of my talk. The woman was attentive during my talk and seemed genuinely interested in why I would choose to become a priest. I started to give her a serious answer, which was going to be somewhat detailed. The main point that I was going to make was that I could not completely understand why I had become a priest because in order to understand my vocation I would have to understand myself completely and understand God completely. I do not understand myself completely and I do not understand God completely. What I could say was what was on my conscious mind as I moved toward the priesthood, what my conscious motives were. The dimension of myself that is beyond my understanding, the depth of myself that I can neither understand completely nor articulate verbally must have had some role in my choice of the priesthood and that will remain a mystery until I meet God. Shortly after I started to try to comment on the mystery of vocation, the woman lost interest and changed the subject!

If a life commitment is mysterious even to a person who makes one, then it is certainly mysterious to someone who is observing it from the outside. One Catholic philosopher claimed that commitments could not be judged from the outside. I suspect that a person who has chosen to make a life commitment to another person is in a situation similar to mine in relation to the priesthood. The person could say what it was about the future spouse that was initially attractive or what about the other's personality was and perhaps still is appealing but I don't think the individual could explain clearly or completely why he or she chose the other as a partner for life.

My own opinion is that God enters into all successful life commitments. The Catholic existentialist philosopher Gabriel Marcel argued for the existence of God from the fact that people enter marriage and make unconditional vows to one another. His argument was that it makes no sense to make an unconditional vow to someone who is human, dependent, finite and weak. It just does not make sense to make a lifelong commitment to someone who can change and let you down. It is not an intelligent thing to do. The very fact that people make unconditional vows implies that there must be an unconditional Being Who sustains those vows and Who can be trusted to be loyal and supportive. In every marriage three are involved: a man, a woman and God.

I wonder how the fear of life commitments that we find in our society is linked to the fact that we live in a death of God culture. How much does disbelief in God influence the hesitancy of some to make life commitments and of many to keep life commitments? If there were no God then I think so called "trial marriages" would make a great deal of sense. Without God to sustain a life commitment, why make one? Wouldn't it be silly to make one?

Of course the term "trial marriage" is a misnomer. It is impossible to try out a life commitment. The nature of a life commitment involves a gift that is unconditional, that has no strings or conditions attached. An individual can experiment with living with someone but it is impossible to experiment with a marriage. The nature of marriage means that one person is no longer testing the other, that the person has made a life commitment to the other which means a commitment which lasts as long as they both shall live.

I have come to believe that the best way of growing as a person, the best way of maturing, of fulfilling personal potential is through a life commitment. Nothing else has such great power to transform us the way that a life commitment has. In making a life commitment we live out the truth that Jesus articulated in saying that the grain of wheat must die if it is going to live. A life commitment provides a special opportunity for a person to die to self and to live for other. Our life commitments make us who we are in a way that no other choices do.

The meaning of truth and love drives us and gives our lives an urgency. Using St. Paul's clarion call *"caritas urget nos"* (the love of Christ drives us) (2 Cor 5:14), Pope Benedict suggests that discovering the truth about human persons and God's creation drives us to establish authentic fraternity. [2] This is the ground upon which a spirituality can grow and deepen. The light of truth and the force of love is what drives us toward a world community and we are called to this community by the word of God who is Love. [3] It is no easy task to form a community on any level but the Holy Father stresses that every effort should be made to promote a person-based and community-oriented cultural process of world-wide integration that is open to transcendence. [4]

God's Presence to Everyone

Some experiences of dialogue have affected me deeply. Some of these dialogues have taken place in philosophy classes at St. John's University, some in discussion groups with priests, some in a discussion with members of the laity, some with priests with whom I live and some with authors whose writings I have read. "Dialoguing" with great authors is a wonderful experience. One event that happened almost forty years ago that profoundly influenced my view of life was reading Gregory Baum's excellent book *Man Becoming*. Thinking back to when I read the book I can remember how excited I was because of the challenges that Baum's writing presented to me. His book challenged me to alter the way I thought about God, the Church, redemption and holiness. I can recall being stunned by what Baum wrote, even threatened to some extent. However by the time that I finished the book and discussed it with some friends, I felt the book was a prophetic and wonderfully clear statement that presented some of the most important insights and developments in twentieth century Catholic theology.

In his book Baum is honest about his own intellectual journey. He confesses early on in *Man Becoming* that he has undergone an intellectual conversion. He mentions that one of the experiences that changed his way of thinking was working with people who were not Catholic. His experience of their goodness made him change his view of God's redemptive presence in people's lives. This especially interested me because it echoed my own experience as a young priest with people who were not Catholic. Like Baum I had to change my notion of redemption and of holiness. Some of my priest classmates found the goodness of people who were not Catholic, or even agnostic and atheistic, very threatening. I found it encouraging. Reporting his own experience of dealing with people who were not Catholic, Baum wrote:

"Very slowly the conviction took hold of me that there is no radical difference between Christians and non-Christians. The same dynamics take place in everyone, whether inside or outside the Church: people have the same fears, receive the same challenges, come to the same possibilities of transformation and self-destruction. To say that Christians are better than others or live on a more elevated plane does not make sense. While there are indeed great Christian men and women inspired by trust and generosity, following Jesus on the road of simplicity, love and candor, there are also great men and women without religion who have been marvelously transformed into selfless, open and trusting persons. Holiness is as universal as sin." [5]

What Baum was calling attention to, and I think it is very important that Catholics believe this deeply, is that the process of redemption is taking place in the lives of everyone, Catholic, Protestant, Jewish, members of Islam, agnostic and atheist. God is lovingly and redemptively present in the life of every human being. It is not just Catholics who are called to an intimate union with God, to a friendship with God. Everyone is called to that relationship. I think that this should cause us to be both joyful and humble. Neither we nor the Church own God. The Spirit is alive in every person and blows where He wills. This means that everyone has a vocation, that everyone is being called by God into an intimate union. No one is excluded, no one is left out. Of course none of us can judge how close or how distant anyone is from God. I do not even know how close or how distant I am from God. Even with ongoing examinations of conscience, even with the grace received from the sacrament of reconciliation, even with the guidance of a spiritual director, I do not know for certain where I stand with God. How dare I ever judge any other person's relationship with God? I suggest that our attitude might be expressed in the following way: "I know that God is calling me and I hope I am responding generously." When we find goodness in those who are not Catholic we should rejoice at the presence of the Holy Spirit in their lives. I agree completely with Baum's view of redemption and his view of the presence of God to all peoples. Strongly influenced by one of the greatest theologians in the history of Roman Catholicism, Karl

Rahner, Baum presents his view as one which will help Catholics to be humble and also help them to see that God is lovingly present to all people. Rahner's theology has had an enormous influence in the post-Vatican Church but some of the great theologian's writings are not easy to grasp. Baum's clear writing makes some of Rahner's insights more easily accessible. Affirming the uniqueness of the Church, and insisting that the mystery of redemption is universal and not limited to Catholics, Baum says that Jesus Christ has revealed what takes place in every person, that there is a pattern or plan of salvation and it applies to all people. Commenting on his change in attitude and the new way that he thinks of salvation, Baum writes:

"This new doctrinal perspective brought out that human life is the same everywhere: the dynamics of life are identical in every man. On the one hand, he is threatened by sin and self-destruction, and, on the other, he is ever summoned, gratuitously and beyond expectation, to new dimensions of truth and love. No wonder, then, that holiness is present outside the Church as well as within. No wonder that we may meet people within the Church who crush their vitality and disrupt their peace, while we encounter outsiders, with or without religion, in whom new life and joy are constantly being created. Not that Christians are worse than other people. The new doctrinal perspective brings out, rather, that salvation is always and everywhere gratuitous. It happens where it happens. Holiness and creative self-possession are always gifts, the unexpected marvels created over the uncertain ground of self-deception." [6]

The Church and God's Presence

There is no lack of evidence that all of us are threatened by sin and self-destruction. We just need to look around us. In fact we can look at ourselves. I think of so many choices I have made that have not been life-giving. How often I feel like St. Paul must have felt when he wrote that the good that he wanted to do he did not do but the evil that he did not want to do, he did. We can look at people within the Church who do not seem to be growing and at people outside the Church who seem to be very caring, unselfish people. This does not mean that membership in the Church is not important. Nor does it mean that the Church's presence in people's lives is not important. It does however call our attention to the profound truth that the Holy Spirit is present everywhere and that some people outside the Church may be more responsive to the Spirit's presence in their lives than some people within the Church.

I suppose that the reason this view can make Catholics humble is that it reminds us that we do not own the Holy Spirit. The Spirit breathes where He will! God's grace is available, not only through the sacraments of the Church, but everywhere. The redeeming love of God is present in every person's life. This means that every person is being called by God. Not only Catholics are called by God. It is not only priests and religious who have a vocation. Everyone has a vocation. Every person is called to accept an intimate love relationship with God. It is quite possible that some people outside the Church are responding to this vocation more freely and unselfishly than some within the Church.

The Church's presence in the world is crucial because the Church explicitly teaches God's plan of salvation and explicitly celebrates the redeeming life, death and resurrection of Jesus. The Church's teaching and sacraments are enormous blessings in the journey of life. They remind us of God's plan and help us model our lives on Jesus. Those who have received the gift of faith in the Church should respond generously and joyously to God's love. They should also be able to recognize God's loving, redemptive presence in some who do not share their Catholic faith and they should rejoice at that presence.

When people ask whether something is relevant they often want something to have an immediate and obvious application to their lives. I have discovered this attitude in some students. If something is not immediately and easily applicable, then it can be rejected as irrelevant, as having no practical application, as having nothing to do with human living. I think such an attitude breeds superficiality. Yet I cannot dismiss the desire for relevance completely. In relation to the Christian faith there is something good about wanting faith to be relevant. We want faith to make a difference in our lives. There is a popular notion that faith must be blind, that it need not make sense, that it should not be rational. Faith should make sense. Living as a Christian believer is an intelligent and reasonable way to live. To say that Christian faith is reasonable is not to say that it can be proven but rather that it illuminates our experience, makes our experience more meaningful. Christian faith is eminently relevant in that it sheds light on every aspect of our lives. That religion, at least sometimes, has been presented as though it deals with some extraordinary area that is above and beyond human living, some special realm which is sometimes called the supernatural, has made religion seem unrelated and unconnected to the deepest needs, desires and hopes of human beings. Religion should offer a critique of human living, should guide us as we try to live out in our lives the meaning of Jesus' message. Even some who believe that God is Father, Son and Holy Spirit, don't see any relationship between their belief in the Trinity and their lives. But that God is Father means that life has a purpose and a goal, that we are not adrift in a meaningless universe, that we have been called into relationship with a loving God. It means that we are not merely God's creatures but God's sons and daughters. That the Son is the Father's Word spoken to us in Jesus, a Word revealing God's love to us and also revealing what being human means, illuminates our journey on earth. God's Word reveals our goal of risen life. That God is Spirit means that we are not alone but that we have received Christ's life-giving Spirit to guide us and guard us on our journey. We are invited by God to enter into relationship with Father, Son and Spirit, not only beyond the grave but here on earth. God wants an intimate loving relationship with us.

Our Father has called us and made promises to us. God has made a commitment to us. Because of God's call and commitment, we can commit ourselves in love to others. We can do this if we are married, if we are single or if we are celibate. God's call, God's self-gift can free us beyond our wildest imaginings. We can imitate and incarnate God's love in our lives. We can do this by reaching out in love to others. There is so much meaning to Christian faith that it goes beyond our capacity to comprehend completely, but what we do comprehend is more relevant than any other meaning. Saying that God calls us to an intimate loving relationship means for the Christian that God calls us to risen life. The truth that God calls everyone to risen life seems to sum up a great deal of what we believe as Catholic Christians. It really is at the center of our faith. It is also at the center of a spirituality of communion.

There are two paragraphs in *Caritas in Veritate* which are like a mini-course in philosophy and Catholic theology. They express both the depth and clarity of Pope Benedict's thought and can be an excellent stimulus for reflection for anyone interested in grasping the Holy Father's vision. Pointing out that the human creature is defined through interpersonal relations, Benedict notes that the more authentically an individual lives these relations, the more he or she matures. A human person does not establish his or her worth through isolation but rather by placing himself or herself in relation to God and others. These relations have a fundamental value and importance and the Pope insists that this is true not just for an individual but for all people. The human community not only does not absorb the individual but helps him or her grow in maturity and personal identity. Just as neither the family nor the Church submerges individuals, the unity of the global community makes persons more transparent and links peoples and cultures more closely in their dazzling diversity. What makes the Pope's insights especially awesome, inspiring and even mind-boggling is that he links the "inclusion-in-relation" of individuals and peoples to the relationship between the Persons in the Trinity within one divine Substance. The Trinity not only becomes a model but the Pope reminds us that God desires to bring us into the reality of communion that is the Trinity.[7] That desire is the fundamental ingredient upon which a spirituality of communion is based.

Questions for Discussion

1. How is the Holy Spirit the "energy" transforming the ecclesial community?
2. How is a life commitment liberating?
3. How are you aware of the process of redemption in your life and in the lives of people you know?
4. What does it mean to say we don't own the Holy Spirit?
5. Should faith influence us in our daily lives? How?

---

[1] *Caritas in Veritate*, op. cit., sections 2-4.
[2] Ibid., section 20.
[3] Ibid., sections 3-4.
[4] Ibid., section 42.
[5] Gregory Baum, *Man Becoming*, New York: Hessler and Hessler, 1970, pp. VIII-IX.
[6] Ibid., pp. X-XI.
[7] *Caritas in Veritate*, op.cit., section 53.

Chapter 6

Hope

Hope, the Future and the Present

There are several reasons that I am glad that Pope Benedict turned his attention toward the virtue of hope in his second encyclical, *Spe Salvi* or "In Hope We Stand." One is that most of my adult life I have been trying to deepen the virtue of hope. St. John of the Cross claimed that in the evening of our life we will be judged by how we have loved. I agree with the great saint but I think that we should remember that finally we are called to trust in the mercy and love of God—to have hope.

There was a time in my life when all my non-academic reading was focused on the virtue of hope. At the time I was a seminarian and my spiritual director believed that I should flood my consciousness with ideas about trusting in God. He believed correctly that at that time in my life I needed to trust in God, that I needed to see that God was worthy of my hope and trust. Any text that would nourish my hope and encourage me to trust in God, I read. I believe that I still need that type of nourishment. Doubtless many of us do.

Even as I re-read Pope Benedict's thoughts my mind immediately conjures up all the voices in the contemporary world expressing lack of hope, especially in the arts. Contemporary literature, theater and film often depict human life as going nowhere, as basically sound and fury signifying nothing. I think of the Albert Camus' novel *The Fall*. A man spends his life telling of his own fall, his own failure to be courageous and to care about others, trying to move others to face their failure and sinfulness. But in Camus' world there is no savior. The main character in Camus' novel is named Jean-Baptiste, but unlike the original John the Baptist, this prophet has no Messiah to proclaim. His message is that there is failure but no redeemer.

I also think of the plays of Eugene O'Neil, plays that are deeply moving but at times seem to be cries from someone who sees no hope for any salvation. I would say the same about the films of Ingmar Bergman or Woody Allen. In Bergman's and Allen's films there is no love that is more powerful than death. All these artists are very talented people but all of them seem to have relinquished any hope for survival after death. None of them can see any blessing that is more powerful than death. All of them are brilliant but they seem to have given up any hope for a life that transcends earthly existence.

This vision of earthly existence that seems so prevalent in the arts is one reason why Pope Benedict's encyclical seems so timely. Many people have lost faith in a life beyond death so a powerful statement about such a life is most welcome. Pope Benedict has made such a statement. The Risen Christ is the sign that God is trustworthy and we can hope.

At the beginning of Pope Benedict's encyclical on hope, the Holy Father makes a point about hope that I think is especially important to make in the contemporary world. [1] Pope Benedict stresses that hope changes the meaning of the future and also the present for the person who hopes. For the person who hopes the future holds out the possibility for complete fulfillment. Hope tells us that personal existence has a goal, that any disappointments that we have had are not the final word about our lives. In revealing that we are justified in hoping for a final union with God, hope can enable us to see a more profound meaning to human existence and a deeper dignity that people have. Saint Augustine said it succinctly and accurately when he wrote that our hearts are restless until they rest in the Lord.

Belief in the immortality of persons changes profoundly the meaning of personal existence. Hope changes not only the meaning of the future but also the meaning of the present. If life on earth is all that we can expect or hope for then human living is robbed of its richness and human love really is counterfeit. If this earthly existence is all that there is then death wins and love loses.

I believe that whenever anyone loves someone the intention is to love that person forever. It is impossible to intend to love someone for a weekend. In fact someone may love someone only for a weekend but that cannot be the intention when the love relationship begins. Whenever someone sincerely says "I love you" the intention is to love that person always, to never withdraw that love. The richest type of love is unconditional. The lover ought never to put a condition on his or her love. The lover ought never to say "I love you if." At least implicitly every lover says "I love you because you are you." Hope is related to God's unconditional love for us and that love will conquer all obstacles, even death.

We tend to think of the future as something external to us, something that happens to us that we have little or no control over. It is similar to the way that we think of the weather, something which we have little influence over and must just accept. I think this is an incorrect way to look at the future. Of course we cannot control whether it rains or snows and we have no control over when or how we die. But we do have significant influence over *whom* it rains or snows on, and significant influence on *who* dies. By our free choices we create ourselves or better we co-create ourselves along with God. I am who I am because of God's free choice and my free choices. Of course there have been many external influences in my life ranging from family and friends to schools and the Church. But the bottom line is I am who I am because I have made free choices. I believe that this is true of most adults.

Because I am creating myself by my free choices I have significant influence over the meaning of my future. I do not control external events but I do choose the person who experiences those events. In that sense I create my future because I create the person who is moving into the future and who will experience future events. In commenting on how hope can make an enormous difference in how a person lives, the Holy Father notes that while hope does not give us a clear image of life beyond the grave, we know that our lives will not end in emptiness.

We should read the gospel differently than we read other material. There is a temptation to reduce the gospel to an interesting piece of literature. We might look upon it as merely informative and we may have lost a sense of urgency and the sense that we are being called to make a decision, even to make a commitment. It is very fitting that at the celebration of the Eucharist we stand when the gospel is being proclaimed. Standing, we are ready to take action. Hearing the Word of God, we stand so that we are prepared to respond, not just mentally but with some action. The Danish father of existentialist philosophy, Soren Kierkegaard, wrote a two-volume work entitled *Either/Or*. He claimed that every book he wrote was written under the sign either/or. By that he meant, I think, that every book he wrote was a challenge to the reader. Kierkegaard in effect was saying to the reader "Either agree with me or find another way." I think of Kierkegaard as a Christian apostle whose writing was calling readers to witness to Christ. It seems to me that the gospel also presents to the reader an either/or challenge. The gospel is not merely an interesting story about a preacher and healer who lived two thousand years ago. The gospel is the proclamation of Jesus as the Savior and Redeemer of the human race. We are called to take a stance in relation to Jesus, to make a decision in relation to Jesus. When we hear the gospel or read the gospel it is not just that we are being exposed to some interesting ideas about Jesus. We have an opportunity to encounter the living Christ.

The Pope insists that the gospel is not only informative in the sense that it reveals previously unknown content. The gospel is performative, which means that it calls us to act, to live in a different way, to change our lives, to convert. [2] As the Holy Father suggests, the gospel can be life-changing. If we take the gospel seriously, then we will be challenged. We ought to resist the temptation to think that the gospel is not good news because we already know the story. Each exposure to the gospel is an opportunity, not only to think about Jesus, but to allow our relationship with the Risen Christ to deepen. The gospel will always be good news if we are receptive. We may have heard the gospel proclaimed many times but still we have a golden opportunity to allow the gospel to deepen our hope.

One of the most attractive characteristics of the encyclical for me is the way that the Pope's understanding of hope permeates the entire letter. While reading *Spe Salvi*, I felt as though I was reading words from a person of deep faith and active hope. I was also reading words from a person who urgently wanted to communicate what he believed to be true to others. I had the feeling that the Holy Father was speaking to me. His writing is provocative, insightful and inspiring. I found especially inspiring the Pope's insistence that it is ultimately not the laws of matter that govern the universe but a Spirit that has revealed himself as Love. At the root of reality there is a Spirit Who is Love! What could be more beautiful or inspiring? What could be more consoling?

I have a vivid recollection of a trip to The Museum of Natural History in Manhattan that another professor from St. John's University and I made about five years ago. We watched a show about the planets and stars that ran for about seventeen minutes and was narrated by Tom Hanks. The solar system was simulated on the ceiling of a darkened auditorium. As we listened to Hanks' comments on the size of the universe, we were in awe at the knowledge that astronomers now have about the universe. Until I heard Hanks' lecture I did not know that the Big Bang Theory claims that once the entire universe was the size of a grain of sand. Amazing! When the show was finished, the other professor and I left the Museum. The exit to the street is by way of a winding ramp that requires walking for three or four minutes. As we walked down the ramp neither the other professor nor I spoke. We were overwhelmed by the show. We were literally speechless. When we finally reached the street I think I said "Wow!" The first thought that occurred to me while watching the show was "How can we matter in such a vast universe? We are just specks, just passing insignificant moments in the history of creation." But then, almost immediately, I thought "The God Who is creating this magnificent universe is totally in love with me. This is almost incredible. Why should such a powerful, intelligent, eternal Being get involved with me? Care about me?" The only answer that I can come up with is that love does such things. Love wants to share. Love calls us into communion.

The other thought that came to me was about Jesus' death on the cross. In this vast universe created by Divine Love it is revealed that I am so important, so significant that the Son of God died for me. Mind boggling! Not only for me but for all people! If we wanted to state the most radical truth about a person, the most profound truth about a person beyond the person's height, weight, skin pigmentation, nationality, I.Q. and sexual orientation, that truth would be that God is totally and completely in love with that person.

Sometimes we can feel abandoned, alone in the universe. Much of contemporary media seems to depict human life as a journey that is frustrating, disappointing and aimlessly going in no direction. The Holy Father's letter meets this view head on and states powerfully that the final word about both the universe and our human existence in the universe is Love. I think that we have to make that profound truth about all creation but especially about us as real to ourselves as we possibly can. I know I need to do that. Whatever else we learn about the human person, the final word and most important word is God's and that Word has revealed that at the root of all created reality is Love.

Heaven and Communion

A criticism sometimes made about Christians is that their interest in the future, specifically in getting into heaven, makes it impossible for them to be real citizens of this world. The criticism suggests that Christians will always have their eyes "on the prize" and passively allow all sorts of evil to continue on this earth because their real interest is in being saved. Some secularists accuse Christians of neglecting the present for the sake of the future, of being preoccupied with the future life at the expense of the present life. Some secularists believe that whatever vision of the future a person has, that view of the future should enrich and nourish the person's present existence. I agree that our vision of the future should enrich and benefit us in living in the present but how does our hope do this? Doesn't hope which is focused on the future necessarily cause us to neglect the present with all its distractions and disappointments? I think Pope Benedict's encyclical on hope is a strong statement about how Christians should view the future and what its relation to the present should be. [3] Nothing that the Pope writes in the letter suggests or encourages a withdrawal from the present world. Rather our hope for the future gives the present a deeper meaning. Hope for the future is based on the presence of Christ in our lives in the present. It is faith in Christ's living presence with us now that frees us to hope for fulfillment in the future. The presence of Christ liberates us so that we can be people of hope, people who trust in the ultimate victory of the Risen Lord. This looking toward the ultimate victory when there will be no more sin or death, when our loving God will wipe every tear from our eyes, not only should not distract us from the problems and suffering of people but should immerse us more deeply in those problems, should move us to be more loving, caring and active in serving people.

The caricature of the follower of Christ as withdrawn from the world, as immune from the problems of the world is just that, a caricature. [4] Wherever and whenever people are suffering, followers of the crucified God should care and should be present in any way that they can. No one of us can do everything but each one of us can do something. Belief in the future, belief in the promises of Christ should not make us disinterested observers of the contemporary world but rather should remind us that those who are suffering are people for whom Christ died. The hope that animates us, though deeply personal, should never be private or turn us away from those in need. A spirituality of communion means that others are our brothers and sisters in Christ.

In his novel *The Plague* atheistic existentialist philosopher Albert Camus portrays a priest as less interested than an atheistic doctor in the suffering of people. The presumption in the story seems to be that faith and hope, because they point to a life beyond the grave, weaken an individual's interest in persons who are suffering in this world. Rather the opposite should be the case. Faith and hope should increase our sense of the preciousness and value of persons and should call us to a love of people even deeper than the love motivated by an atheistic vision. The human mind, unaided by faith and hope, can discover that persons have a special value; the mind enlightened by faith and hope can grasp that the value of persons is expressed by the great price paid for their salvation, namely the death and resurrection of Jesus.

The Holy Father comments that for some people images of eternal life are not attractive, in fact are completely unappealing. What many people want, says the Holy Father, is not eternal life but present life. To them living for ever, living endlessly, appears more like a curse than a gift. Having noted how difficult it is to imagine eternal life, Pope Benedict comments that even the term "eternal life" is inadequate and can cause confusion. He says that "eternal" can suggest something interminable and "life" can include those aspects of our experience that we love but also those aspects that we find very difficult. The Holy Father suggests we imagine heaven as plunging into an ocean of infinite love. [5] Of course no one can imagine what heaven is really like but I do like what the Holy Father has written. It would seem that whatever form existence in heaven takes, it must be "the supreme moment of satisfaction." The idea and image of plunging into the ocean of infinite love speaks to me. I cannot completely understand what this might mean but what I know of love suggests to me that this is one of the better ways to imagine heaven.

Images of people in white robes walking among the clouds do not seem a very good depiction of heavenly existence. Playing harps does not seem like a very interesting way to spend eternity. Even the notion that heaven is somewhere high in the sky does not speak to me. I am a little surprised how long some depictions of heaven stay in people's consciousness and influence the way they think of eternal life. I once met a very intelligent and well-educated writer who thought that a Catholic believed that if I got into a plane and flew up high enough I would see God on a cloud!

If our earthly existence can tell us anything about heaven then heaven must be some kind of intensification of our experience of love. [6] We believe that God is Love and so heaven, being fulfilled with God, would seem to be best imagined, however inadequately, as some kind of fulfillment of love. However mysterious heavenly existence is, it would seem that since loving and being loved are the most fulfilling human experiences on earth that heaven would be something like those experiences. If we can move past most images of heaven that we received when we were children and link our notions of heaven to some kind of fulfillment related to the presence of God Who is Love, we will not understand heaven completely but we may find that we imagine heaven as a more satisfying place than one in which we wear white robes and play harps! Probably rather than trying to imagine heaven we should just trust that God is going to bless us beyond our imaginings.

Pope Benedict raises an important question about whether hope is individualistic or social. [7] Certainly no one can hope in the place of someone else and so there is a sense in which only an individual can hope for himself or herself. No one can substitute for someone else.

However this is not the final word and may not even be the most important word about hope. This virtue definitely has a social dimension. Because of re-reading the Holy Father's letter, I think I see more clearly and more deeply just how social hope is.

I think with a little reflection we can get some sense of how much we are influenced and affected by others. It is probably impossible to emphasize too much the influence that our parents have on us. Think of the teachers and schoolmates that have influenced us profoundly. I have vivid memories of the Sisters who taught me in grammar school and of the Jesuit priests and laymen who taught me in high school. I can only guess how much the priests who taught me when I was a seminarian influenced me. I suspect that each of us can look at our lives and get a sense that to some extent who we are is the result of those who have had a powerful effect on us. I believe that spending time with people who place their trust in God can influence us deeply. People who hope in God, at least indirectly, call us to hope. Their trust in God encourages us to trust in God.

There is a strong personalist strain to some parts of the Holy Father's letter. He stresses that we are called to be open to others and to change the world. The tendency toward self-centeredness and selfishness is strong in many of us but to surrender to this tendency really does put us into a "prison." It locks us in and prevents us from growing. When we become receptive and open to others, we have an opportunity to be liberated. The presence of other persons can call us beyond our narrow self-interests, can broaden and deepen our perception of what is and what is not important.

While our hope is centered on God and is directed beyond this present world that does not mean that it does not have a role in this world or that it will not make a difference here and now. A community of hope will move its members to do what is possible to make the world better, to help people change and even to transform structures. I very much like Pope Benedict's comment that the building up of this world will take place in many different ways. Not only will it depend on historical context but it will also depend on people's intelligence, commitment and zeal. No one can do everything but everyone can do something. We should never minimize the importance of any efforts that we make to help people or to make the world better. Whatever we do can be used by the Holy Spirit in ways beyond our imagination. We try our best and leave the rest to the Spirit.

Hope and Freedom

In recent years I have come to think of freedom as the most precious of gifts but also the gift from God that makes human living such a risky business. In giving us freedom God has taken a chance on us. In a sense God has put Himself at our mercy. Once God creates freedom God relinquishes complete control over us. We are capable of disappointing God, of not doing God's will. Among all God's creatures on this earth only human persons have this power. Freedom really is awesome.

Several events in my life have helped me appreciate freedom in new ways. In reading and teaching philosophy I have spent a great deal of time with the ideas of existentialist philosophers such as Jean Paul Sartre, Albert Camus and Martin Heidegger and personalist philosophers such as Martin Buber, Gabriel Marcel, Emmanuel Mounier and John Mac Murray. Freedom is central to the philosophical visions of each of these thinkers. Also influential in my understanding of the central role of freedom in human existence is my own effort to live a Christian life and my observation as a priest of the efforts of others to live Christian lives. After re-reading Pope Benedict's encyclical *Spe Salvi*, I have come to see in a new way how hope and freedom go together.

In his letter the Pope criticizes Karl Marx for overlooking the importance of human freedom. [8] The Holy Father believes that Marx thought that if all economic needs were met, if we lived in a society in which there were no rich and no poor, then a perfect world would have been reached. Benedict points out that because of human freedom there can be no guarantee concerning human activity. People are free and that means that they can choose the bad rather than the good, sin rather than what is moral, evil rather than what will benefit people.

Some people tend to think that they are pawns in society, unable to direct their lives. The Holy Father stresses that human freedom is always fragile and that the kingdom of good will never be perfectly achieved on earth. He also stresses that anyone who assures people that a better world is guaranteed is forgetting human freedom.

I once had an interesting discussion with a philosopher who has spent the last fifty years of his life trying to find some answer to life's problems, some vision that he can wholeheartedly embrace. I said to him "If I say that God is Love and that we are called to love God and to love one another what would you find objectionable in that view of life?" He said that if this were true then things are supposed to be getting better and they don't seem to be getting better. I said "What do you mean by 'supposed'? Who says they are supposed to be getting better? If we are free then our free actions may be making matters worse rather than better. We can freely do what is wrong."

Hope liberates us so that we can reach a new level of freedom. Because of our belief in God's love for us we can give ourselves away in service to others. Hope enables us to make a life commitment, to gamble our lives on God's love for us. The secret to human happiness and to human fulfillment is reaching out in love to others, our families, our friends but also others in various ways.

All of us have in our lives hoped for many different things. Probably our hopes when we were younger differed from our hopes later in life. What seems to be a universal human experience is that as soon as a hope is fulfilled we realize that this hope was not the final hope and that the reality for which we hoped is not the reality that will fulfill our deepest desires and our deepest needs. Some contemporary thinkers believe that our deepest desires and needs will never be fulfilled and so conclude that human living is absurd. They echo Shakespeare's MacBeth that "Life is sound and fury signifying nothing."

Someone has described the experience of getting what you desire as the "melancholy of fulfillment," meaning that no sooner is our desire fulfilled than we experience something of a letdown or at least realize that we have to look elsewhere for complete fulfillment.

Pope Benedict in his encyclical has a number of wonderful insights into hope in relation to our needs and desires. What is especially appealing I think is that though the Holy Father is dealing with profound mysteries, he

writes clearly. One example of his ability to present clearly what he wishes to say is what he writes about greater
and lesser hopes. [9] Asceticism and prayer can help us to
keep our desires and needs properly focused. If our
prayer life involves us in a deep relationship with God,
we probably will come to see more and more clearly that
only God is our fulfillment. To see this deeply may take a
lifetime for some of us. Perhaps it is a gradual seeing more
into who we are and what our desires are and a gradual
entering more and more into God's life. In the contem-
pory world a prevalent outlook concerning the vows of
poverty, chastity and obedience which members of religious orders take, is that they narrow a person's life and
shrink a person's vision of life and possibilities but this
view is completely erroneous. What is supposed to happen to a person who takes the three vows, in fact to anyone who takes vows for life, such as one takes in marriage,
is that their life becomes richer and they see better what is
most important in human living.

Obviously there is a sense in which a vow limits a person. Someone who takes a vow of chastity cannot marry,
someone who takes a marriage vow should not relate
romantically to someone other than his or her spouse.
However those vows free someone to enter into life in a
special way. Whatever limits a vow places on an individual's life cannot compare to the freedom that the
vowed person can experience through the vow. A vow
opens up a new way of relating. Baptismal vows do this,
marriage vows do this and vows that religious make do
this. In relation to the virtue of hope, vows can focus people, give their life a unity and direction. Any false hopes
that the media or society present should be less likely to

seduce someone who is trying to place his or her hope in God.

There are probably different sections of Pope Benedict's encyclical on hope that will speak to readers more powerfully than other sections. This is probably true of everything that we read. One section of the Pope's letter that jumped off the page at me was a section in which the Holy Father offers some ideas about hope and prayer. [10] In my own life I think that during the last few years I have come to see in new ways the power of prayer to lead people more deeply into relationship with God. When we are attentive in prayer we meet God so to speak "face to face." Our lives are surrounded by the presence of God, but in formal prayer we step into a special space and time in which we focus our attention and love on the Presence Who is always lovingly present to us. The Holy Father writes beautifully but simply about God's presence to us when we pray. The Pope notes that prayer provides an essential setting for learning to hope. He points out that when no one else listens to us, God will listen to us; when there is no one to talk to or call upon, we can talk to God; when there is no one to help us deal with needs, God can help us. Stressing that prayer is not an escape or withdrawal from history into some private corner of happiness, but rather an entering more deeply into life, an opening both to God and to others, Pope Benedict sees prayer as an activity that can both challenge and purify our consciences. Prayer helps us to see that all people have a common Father, Who loves all beyond our comprehension.

I love the idea that in opening ourselves to God in prayer we are allowing God to challenge our consciences.

In reflecting on the dialogue between God and us that constitutes prayer, I think of the presence of two friends to one another. Imagine a deep conversation between two people who are close friends or even married to each other. What takes place in such a conversation often goes beyond the words spoken or the words heard. There can be something happening that almost seems magical. The loving presence of each to the other can go beyond what words can express. In such a conversation people can be deeply moved and profoundly affected. Such conversations can deepen our appreciation of love and even can challenge our consciences. In such conversations we, at least sometimes, are called to see reality differently, to appreciate what we may have taken for granted.

Something similar to what can happen between two close friends in a deep conversation can happen between God and us in prayer but what can happen between God and us is more wonderful. Being lovingly receptive to God's presence to us when we pray can allow God to touch us with love and to heal and expand our consciences. If close friends can help us to see what is most important then God can do that and more.

The poet E.E. Cummings wrote "Be of love a little more careful than of anything." I presume that he was alluding to the truth that love can change our life dramatically. Open yourself to the love that someone offers you and your life may change dramatically. Open yourself to the love that God offers and your life will change dramatically. Hope is at the center of a Christian life. Prayer can help us both to see that and to hope. Be of prayer a little more careful than of anything. Prayer can change us dramatically. It can open us up to communion.

Questions for Discussion

1. What in society makes it difficult to hope?
2. What in society aids hope?
3. How do we "control" the future?
4. How has Pope Benedict's writing on heaven affected your understanding of it?
5. Is the Christian message "informative" or "performative" or neither or both?
6. In prayer how does God challenge our conscience?

---

[1] *Spe Salvi*, section 2.
[2] Ibid., section 10.
[3] Ibid., section 15.
[4] Ibid., section 25.
[5] Ibid., section 12.
[6] Ibid., section 28.
[7] Ibid., section 13.
[8] Ibid., sections 20-21.
[9] Ibid., section 31.
[10] Ibid., sections 32-34.

Conclusion

There is no aspect of human living that cannot be included in and illuminated by a spirituality of communion. It is all inclusive. Everything that Christians believe about God, about themselves and about other human persons not only fits into a spirituality of communion but takes on a deeper meaning, a meaning that is awesome and that challenges Christians to actions.

A spirituality of communion is rooted in the history of God's dealings with people. God is radical mystery and will never be completely comprehended by a finite human mind. God is always more and better than any statement made about God. Yet we are not in the dark with our own groping reflection on the mystery of the Divine. God has spoken and acted in history.

A spirituality of communion is based on the Triune God's calling human persons into a love relationship—all human persons. The early Christians experienced God not only as beyond them as Father but also as with them as Christ and within them as Spirit. A spirituality of communion encourages Christians to relate to God as the Triune God relates to us.

In trying to imitate God who is pure self-gift, Christians are called to reach out to others in any way they can by witnessing in word and deed God's unfathomable love for all human beings. This witness can be incarnated in an almost infinite number of ways. Some will be more formal and structured such as getting involved in some official ministry within the Christian community, some will be less formal and more spontaneous and will come about in various circumstances and events just because of the believer's Christian commitment and his or her witnessing to that commitment in daily life.

The Eucharist is the meal that forms and shapes communion. It makes the Risen Christ sacramentally present and calls worshipers to prayer and action. It expresses liturgically the meaning of communion with God and with others and enables Christians to believe that they share in Christ's powerful conquest of sin and to hope and trust that they will share in His victory over death.

There are many problems in the contemporary world. No one person can solve all of them but everyone can be a channel for good because of God's involvement with us. A spirituality of communion encourages us to reach out in love toward others and to believe and trust that God's love insures ultimate victory.

MAGNETIZED BY GOD
Religious Encounters through Film, Theater, Literature and Art
Robert E. Lauder

"... he suggests that in great art God may be reaching out to us and through our experience of great art we may be able to encounter God."

—*Liv Ullmann*

No. RP 132/04 ISBN 1-878718-92-1   **$8.95**

REACHING OUT
How to Communicate Gospel Hope and Love to 21st Century Catholics
Joseph B. Lynch, S.M.

"*Thoughtful, practical and motivating,* Reaching Out *is a resource parish leaders will welcome and consult often.*"

—*Maureen Jessnik RSM*

No. RP 754/04 ISBN 1-933066-08-0   **$9.95**

THE NINE HABITS OF HIGHLY EFFECTIVE CHRISTIANS
Victor M. Parachin

"*Parachin's easy-to-read primer on how to be a better Christian is filled with anecdotes, examples, and tips for Christian action and has something for everyone.*"

—*Marci Alborghetti*

No. RP 757/04 ISBN 1-933066-11-0   **$6.95**

FEASTS OF LIFE
Recipes from Nana's Wooden Spoon
Father Jim Vlaun

"*Filled with wonderful stories and even better-sounding recipes in seven categories . . . The dishes are easy to make and don't require fancy ingredients—just good, old-fashioned meats, cheese and vegetables. . . . Includes a prayer for grace, a cooking equivalents table and a cross-referenced index.*" —*Crux of the News*

No. RP 168/04 ISBN 1-878718-76-2   **$12.95**

www.catholicbookpublishing.com

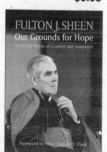

Additional Titles Published by Resurrection Press, a Catholic Book Publishing Imprint

A Rachel Rosary *Larry Kupferman*	$4.50
A Season in the South *Marci Alborghetti*	$10.95
Blessings All Around *Dolores Leckey*	$8.95
Catholic Is Wonderful *Mitch Finley*	$4.95
Days of Intense Emotion *Keeler/Moses*	$12.95
The Edge of Greatness *Joni Woelfel*	$9.95
Feasts of Life *Jim Vlaun*	$12.95
From Holy Hour to Happy Hour *Francis X. Gaeta*	$7.95
5-Minute Miracles *Linda Schubert*	$4.95
Grace Notes *Lorraine Murray*	$9.95
Healing through the Mass *Robert DeGrandis, SSJ*	$9.95
Healing Your Grief *Ruthann Williams, OP*	$7.95
Heart Peace *Adolfo Quezada*	$9.95
How Shall We Pray? *James Gaffney*	$5.95
The Joy of Being an Altar Server *Joseph Champlin*	$5.95
The Joy of Being a Catechist *Gloria Durka*	$4.95
The Joy of Being a Eucharistic Minister *Mitch Finley*	$5.95
The Joy of Being a Lector *Mitch Finley*	$5.95
The Joy of Being an Usher *Gretchen Hailer, RSHM*	$5.95
The Joy of Music Ministry *J.M. Talbot*	$6.95
The Joy of Praying the Rosary *James McNamara*	$5.95
The Joy of Preaching *Rod Damico*	$6.95
The Joy of Teaching *Joanmarie Smith*	$5.95
The Joy of Worshiping Together *Rod Damico*	$5.95
Life, Love and Laughter *Jim Vlaun*	$7.95
Lights in the Darkness *Ave Clark, O.P.*	$8.95
Loving Yourself for God's Sake *Adolfo Quezada*	$5.95
Meditations for Survivors of Suicide *Joni Woelfel*	$8.95
Mother O' Mine *Harry W. Paige*	$9.95
Mother Teresa *Eugene Palumbo, S.D.B.*	$5.95
Mourning Sickness *Keith Smith*	$8.95
Our Grounds for Hope *Fulton J. Sheen*	$7.95
Praying the Lord's Prayer with Mary *Muto/vanKaam*	$8.95
Sabbath Moments *Adolfo Quezada*	$6.95
Season of New Beginnings *Mitch Finley*	$4.95
Sometimes I Haven't Got a Prayer *Mary Sherry*	$8.95
St. Katharine Drexel *Daniel McSheffery*	$12.95
What He Did for Love *Francis X. Gaeta*	$5.95
Woman Soul *Pat Duffy, OP*	$7.95
You Are My Beloved *Mitch Finley*	$10.95

For a free catalog call 1-800-892-6657
www.catholicbookpublishing.com